SPACE SCIENCE
PROJECTS FOR YOUNG SCIENTISTS

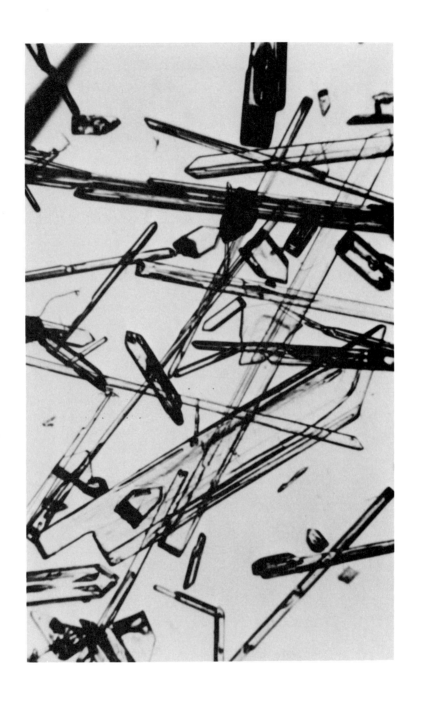

DAVID W. MCKAY
BRUCE G. SMITH

SPACE SCIENCE PROJECTS FOR YOUNG SCIENTISTS

A GROLIER COMPANY

PROJECTS FOR YOUNG SCIENTISTS
FRANKLIN WATTS
NEW YORK I LONDON I TORONTO I SYDNEY

FRONTISPIECE: SPACE-GROWN CRYSTALS.

Diagrams by Vantage Art

Photographs courtesy of: The 3M Company: frontis-
piece, p. 65; NASA: pp. 10, 16, 18, 21, 27, 31, 39, 55,
57, 61, 62, 76, 78, 81, 89, 92, 97, 101, 107; Roger F.
Kerstner: pp. 25, 28, 33, 45, 53, 70; Mount Wilson and
Las Campanas Observatories, Carnegie Institution of
Washington: p. 48; The Yerkes Observatory: p. 49.

Library of Congress Cataloging-in-Publication Data

McKay, David W.
Space science.
(Projects for young scientists)
Bibliography: p.
Includes index.
Summary: Ideas and instructions for a variety of
science projects that examine the characteristics of
the space environment and consider forces such as
gravity, magnetism, and buoyancy.
1. Space sciences—Experiments—Juvenile literature.
(1. Space sciences—Experiments. 2. Experiments)
I. Smith, Bruce G. II. Title. III. Series.
QB500.264.M36 1986   500.5′07′8   86-7745
ISBN 0-531-15134-4 (paper ed.)
ISBN 0-531-10244-0 (lib. ed.)

CONTENTS

SPACE SCIENCE
PROJECTS FOR YOUNG SCIENTISTS

1

OPPORTUNITY AND CHALLENGE

As you sit reading this book, the chances are good that astronauts are orbiting the earth in vehicles such as the American space shuttle or the Russians' Soyuz space-craft. These men and women were sent into space to make observations of the earth and/or space, launch and retrieve satellites, test various pieces of equipment, and do other jobs.

Among the most important of these jobs is to conduct experiments on materials and organisms that cannot be done in a laboratory on the surface of the earth. A vehicle orbiting the earth provides a near-weightless environment as well as a position high above most of the atmosphere. A normal space shuttle orbit is about 140 miles (225 kilometers, or km) in altitude. A weightless environment effectively has no gravitational force.

Experiments conducted in space are leading to exciting new discoveries about our universe and even to some practical applications. For example, it may be possible to manufacture certain drugs in space that are more pure than if they were manufactured on earth.

Space flight thus provides a unique opportunity to expand what we know about the universe and how things in it behave.

Perhaps you have been on a camping trip and sat around a warm fire on a cool summer night. As you watch the flames, you occasionally look at the area around the

The dawning of the shuttle age:
the space shuttle Columbia, STS-1

camp. The only light provided is the flickering light of the burning logs. You can see only a relatively short distance into the surrounding area, and even that view is distorted by the wavering light source.

Imagine how limited your knowledge of the world would be if this were the only way you could gather information about it. What things would you never even have a chance to learn about? What things would you have a distorted view of? For example, what is really on the other side of those trees? If you get up from the fire and venture into the area around the fire and then into the whole vast world around you, imagine the new knowledge you would gain. This is the kind of opportunity provided by orbital vehicles and by space probes.

There was a time when space exploits could only be imagined or fantasized through reading science fiction novels or watching Buck Rogers serials. Now, real-life adventures have been embarked upon by Mercury, Gemini, Soyuz, Apollo, Mariner, Luna, Voyager, Skylab, and the space shuttle Columbia, to name just a few of the vehicles sent from earth to explore space.

The astronauts and cosmonauts who have flown and are flying in the various space programs were probably like you when they were young—inquisitive and interested in learning about new things. They were excited about the idea of exploring a new environment—space. The advantage you have is that your prospects of actually exploring or working in space, or working on space-related projects, are much better. The foundation has been laid, and more opportunities exist today than in the past.

SPACE SCIENCE PROJECTS

This book provides you with information and ideas for doing projects in space science. In doing these projects you will, hopefully, get a clearer picture of the nature of the space environment.

Some projects in this book demonstrate the possibilities and limitations of the types of experiments performed on the space shuttle, satellites, space stations, or deep space probes. Other projects try to simulate the conditions in space. Still others help you understand the forces acting upon things on the earth, such as gravity and magnetism. In turn, this should enable you to visualize the effect of a lack of these forces on materials and organisms.

Because you probably won't have time to do all of these projects, you can do some of them as "thought experiments." In other words, once you have an understanding of the forces acting in space, you can visualize the experiment and try to guess the outcome. For several of the projects that you do, you will need to obtain special kinds of equipment or supplies. Appendix Three lists some sources of these items.

PLANNING THE PROJECTS

As with any job, it is important to have a plan of action, an outline of what you want to accomplish, and a good method of going about getting it done. The job of a space scientist is to discover why and how things behave the way they do in the universe. On occasion, things of great importance are discovered by luck or chance. More often, however, scientific discoveries are made possible by planning, study, and plain hard work. A scientist trying to understand a particular phenomenon needs a plan of attack. One type of plan is the scientific method.

The scientific method is a logical way of approaching problems that has evolved over centuries of scientific study. It is a sequence of stages that helps you organize how you obtain new information and make new discoveries about the universe. Using the scientific method is a good way to tackle the projects in this book and a way to ensure that your observations and conclusions are valid.

The scientific method has four essential stages, and although a scientist may not go through the stages in the same order during an experiment, each is important to the discovery of new information. The four stages are observation, hypothesis, experimentation, and retesting.

OBSERVATION
Observation involves collecting information, or data. As you study something more carefully, you begin to organize and classify your information. Some of the data you collect may prove to be important, but some of it may be meaningless. At this point you can't tell the difference between an important observation and an unimportant observation, so it is vital to collect as much information as you can.

HYPOTHESIS
A *hypothesis* is an educated guess at how or why a particular phenomenon occurs. A hypothesis has to be testable by experiment. Scientists use hypotheses to help guide them in developing experiments. You will use them in planning how you will perform a particular project and what you want to learn from it.

EXPERIMENTATION
Next you look for a way to support or disprove the hypothesis. The hypothesis should lead directly to an experiment related to the hypothesis. An experiment may be simple or extremely complex. It is important, however, that the experiment test only one condition or characteristic at a time and not a lot of different things.

For example, let's say you want to determine how a space flight may affect a mouse. Rather than just launching the animal and seeing whether it survives, you would obtain much more valid and useful data by limiting the focus of the experiment. You could test the effect of rapid acceleration on the heart rate of the animal. In this way you could determine a very specific cause-and-effect relationship.

In an experiment, the specific characteristics that you observe are called *variables*. In the example above, the variables are (1) the rate of acceleration and (2) the

SAFETY

- **Make safety your top priority.** The information on this page and elsewhere in this book will help you accomplish this aim. Instructions and safety cautions are based on recent, reliable information but cannot possibly cover all possible situations. You must exercise your own good judgment and rely on that of your teacher.

- **Do ALL experiments under supervision of a science teacher.**

- **Follow instructions and heed safety cautions.** If in doubt, check with the teacher. Work carefully. A careless or apathetic attitude toward safety may lead to a serious accident. Knowledge and preparation are the keys to controlling hazards.

- **Protect your eyes, ears, face, hands, and body while conducting experiments. WEAR SAFETY GOGGLES OR A FACE SHIELD AT ALL TIMES.** Wear earplugs if your project may be noisy. Wear gloves and a plastic apron to protect your hands and body against spills.

- **Be especially careful while working with chemicals.** Many chemicals are poisonous or flammable or give off irritating fumes. (Don't wear contact lenses!) Work in a well-ventilated area and wash your hands and all equipment after you are through working with the chemicals. Never touch or taste chemicals.

- **Keep your work space neat and organized.** Sloppiness can lead to accidents.

- **Know where you can get help fast in case of an emergency.**

heart rate of the mouse. The variable that you can directly control is called the *independent variable*. In our example, we will control the acceleration. The phenomenon that you observe is called the *dependent variable*. You control the dependent variable only indirectly. Many projects attempt to establish the relationship between two variables in this way.

In space, gravity, atmosphere, and the earth's magnetic field are either absent or diminished in force or density These are the variables the space scientist strives to understand.

MODIFYING THE
HYPOTHESIS AND RETESTING
Often the result of an experiment may not completely support the hypothesis you had when you started the experiment. A good scientist is always ready to modify his or her present idea of how things work based on new information or experimental results. This is the heart and essence of science. A hypothesis becomes a *theory* and is valid only so long as it withstands these challenges and retesting. Much of the work done by scientists is to repeat previously done experiments to ensure their validity.

ARISTOTLE VERSUS GALILEO

Let's go through the scientific process to try to learn about a subject of vital importance to the space scientist: the effect of gravity on falling bodies. You can use this project as a model of how to perform future activities in the book.

You may have noticed that different objects fall at different speeds. If you haven't, go drop two solid objects like a marble and a piece of paper from the same height and see which one falls faster. Does this mean that heavy objects fall faster than light ones? As a thought experiment this seems to make sense, but is it really true?

Let's now increase our experience with falling objects by doing a series of informal experiments.

*Early scientific pio-
neer Galileo Galilei
(1564–1642)*

Collect about six objects around your home that would not be broken or damaged by a short fall, for example, a baseball, basketball, piece of paper, balloon, and a cotton ball or Ping-Pong ball. Try to find objects with different weights, shapes, and textures. Two of the objects should be about the same size but have different weights.

Drop the objects two at a time from the same height, releasing them at the same time. Note which of the two lands first or if they land at the same time. See if you can determine which objects fall faster.

You have just performed an uncontrolled experiment. Little attempt has yet been made to control the various factors or variables that may affect the experiment. What factors do you think are important in how fast an object will fall? Did one of the objects always fall faster than, or at least as fast as, all the other objects? What did that object look like?

You are now ready to form a hypothesis about the nature of falling objects. Can you make a general statement, based on your observations so far, as to which objects fall faster than others?

One hypothesis about falling objects put forth by an early experimenter, Aristotle, was that "heavy things fall faster than light things." He based this hypothesis primarily on thought experiments and common sense. He did not attempt to test the hypothesis through controlled experimentation, but in the following project, we will.

In this experiment, the rate at which an object falls will be our dependent variable. The *mass* of the objects is the independent variable. Design the experiment to vary the mass of objects and observe the rate at which they fall. Didn't we do that already? Yes, but we made no attempt to identify and control any factors other than mass that may affect how fast an object falls.

We must take a more careful look at the objects that we used and the environment in which they were falling and try to identify those factors. For example, do things such as size, shape, texture, or color affect how fast they fall? Since we don't really know, we should try to keep all other possible variables constant. However, this may not be practical, so we should at least identify the ones most likely to affect the rate of falling. Do you really think color will have an effect? Probably not. What about shape? Maybe. Will an object fall at the same rate through water as it will through air?

In this experiment, it is fairly obvious that shape, size, and the medium the objects fall through are the major variables we will want to control.

We must now select two objects to drop that are identical in *all* ways except for their mass. One way this was accomplished by another famous experimenter, Galileo, was by taking two identical balls and filling one with some heavy material so that one was many times heavier than the other. You can do the same thing with two old tennis balls. The following experiment will help you to support or refute Aristotle's hypothesis about falling objects. You will need an assistant.

1. Obtain two old tennis balls that are as identical as you can find. Cut a slit in one ball about 1½ inches (4 centimeters, or cm) long with a knife. Use heavy gloves or hold

*Artist's concept of Pioneer spacecraft over
the famous Red Spot on the planet Jupiter*

the ball in a towel when cutting the slit. Squeeze the ball so that an opening is made. Obtain some sand or dirt. (Salt also works.) Pour as much of the sand or dirt into the tennis ball as you can get into it. Don't fill it too much or the opening won't close. Brush any excess material off the ball. You may want to seal the slit with tape or glue.

2. Find a place to perform the experiment. Choose a place so that you can drop the balls from a height of about 10 feet (3 meters, or m). You may need a chair or stool to stand on. Select a place where the ball can fall and not cause any damage. You may want to put down a pad to cushion the impact of the balls.

3. Ask your assistant to hold the two tennis balls close together (but not touching) at the same height (10 feet). Position yourself so that you can closely observe which of the two balls hits first. Instruct your assistant not to tell you which ball is weighted. Have him or her drop both balls at the same time. Record which ball strikes first or if they hit at the same time. Set up a table or chart to keep track of your results.

4. Repeat the experiment a number of times. To eliminate the possibility that your assistant may not be dropping the balls the same with both hands, it is a good idea to perform the experiment perhaps five times with the weighted ball in the right hand and the other ball in the left hand. Then run the experiment five more times with the balls exchanged. Always record your results as you objectively observe them. Do not prejudge your results.

5. Take a look at your data. Did all the experimental trials show the same results? Was there some definite trend to the results? Do the results support or refute Aristotle's hypothesis? Suggest another hypothesis concerning the way that objects fall.

HERE WE GO AGAIN!

You have now gone full cycle in the experimental procedure. You could design another experiment to test the new hypothesis. And so it goes. The study of the things around us and our attempt to gain knowledge is never at an end. It is a self-perpetuating process. New knowledge leads to new questions!

2

MATTER AND ENERGY IN ORBIT

The first human-made objects in space were weather balloons and similar devices, special planes such as the X-1, and rockets. Once an effective way was found to enter space, scientists and engineers could think about keeping objects in space. The results of this technological advance were satellites of various types and manned orbital vehicles.

Objects orbiting the earth manage to stay in orbit because of a balance between the gravitational pull of the earth on the object and the *centripetal force* exerted on the object as it whirls around the earth. Centripetal force is the outward force on an object caused by its rotation around another object. Centripetal force pushes the laundry in a washing machine on "spin" against the sides of the washer. Without centripetal force, a satellite would fall to earth very quickly.

A space probe far away from the earth (or any other heavenly body) will be weightless. A satellite orbiting the earth will also be weightless along with everything inside the satellite, including human beings. In the first case, the probe is too far away for gravity to have much effect; the force of gravity decreases the farther you move from an object. In the second case, the force of gravity is canceled out by the centripetal force. One force pulls one way; the other, the other way. The net result is no force on the satellite.

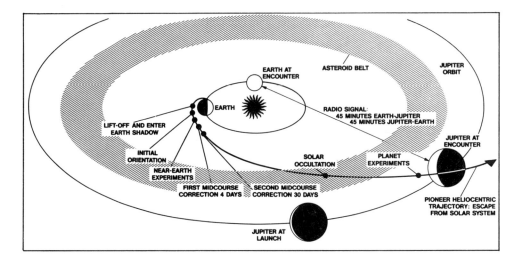

Diagram showing planned launch path of the Pioneer Jupiter spacecraft. Scientists and technicians planning space flights have to consider the various forces acting on the moving spacecraft.

Scientists and engineers have to deal with these matters as well as with the effects of *weightlessness* on human beings. They also have to deal with the electrical-energy demands of satellites, spaceships, and human beings in space. As the space program grows, these needs will be increasing and this will require more sophisticated solutions.

If human beings are to successfully explore and live in space, we must try to thoroughly understand the space environment and the energy requirements of the satellites, probes, spaceships, and human beings within it. The projects in this chapter will start you off in this direction.

MEASURING CENTRIPETAL FORCE

The same laws of motion describe and govern the motion of a satellite or spacecraft in orbit about the

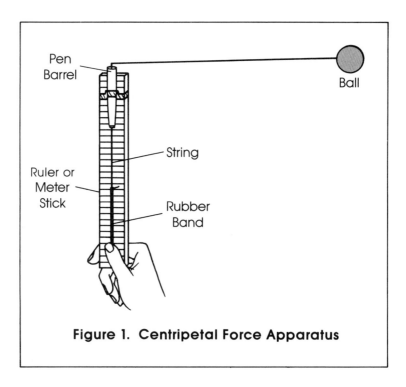

Figure 1. Centripetal Force Apparatus

earth and the motion of an object swung around in the air at the end of a string. In this project, you will investigate satellite motion by working with a ball and string.

The mass and speed of the ball, the length of the string, and the centripetal force are the variables you will be manipulating. Centripetal force in this project is the tension of the string that pulls the object toward the center of rotation. The force will be measured by the amount of stretch of a rubber band. A rubber band stretches and changes its length in a manner approximately proportional to the applied force.

You will need the following materials and equipment: ball-point pen, 3-foot (1-m) wooden ruler, tape, about 6 feet (2 m) of string, rubber band, two rubber balls, metronome.

Take the pen apart and remove the ink cartridge

from it. Tape the pen barrel to one end of the ruler, and run the piece of string through the barrel of the pen. Then tie the rubber band to one end of the string. Attach one rubber ball to the other end of the string. Do not use metal or other hard objects in place of the ball; they are dangerous. See Figure 1.

Hold the apparatus in your right hand and swing the rubber ball around above your head. Hold the end of the rubber band in your left hand. Read the centripetal force in terms of the length of the rubber band. Because the stretch of the rubber band alters the orbit, keep the knot joining the string and the rubber band on the same mark on the ruler at all times.

Move your hand holding the end of the rubber band up and down to keep the knot in the same place. Set the speed of the ball with the metronome, or have an assistant call out times for you. Keep the orbital speed constant by adjusting the speed of the ball until it passes exactly the same point with every tick of the metronome. The orbital speed can be expressed as the number of revolutions the ball makes per second.

Change only one of the variables at a time so that you can find the effect of each variable independently of the others. Two values are enough for each case. Make a table and record the following measurements for each trial: the radius of orbit the object makes, the orbital speed, and the number of balls attached to the string.

Measure how much the rubber band stretches (the *force*) when the orbital speed is kept constant, one rubber ball is used, and the distance is kept constant. Repeat the trial. This is the control, a standard against which other experimental results are measured.

Measure the force when the orbital speed is exactly doubled. Keep everything else the same as in the control. Repeat the trial.

Attach the second rubber ball and again measure the force when the distance and orbital speed are the same as in the control. Repeat the trial. Calculate the swing rate as before.

Remove the second rubber ball, and remove enough string so the orbit is half what it was in the control. Then measure the force when the orbital speed is the same as in the control with one rubber ball. Repeat the trial.

What is the effect on the centripetal force when the mass is doubled and the speed and distance are held constant? What is the effect on the force when the distance is halved and the speed and mass are held constant? What is the effect on force when the speed is doubled and the distance and mass are held constant?

An interesting extension to this project is to gather more data, using other distances, more balls, and different orbital speeds. See if you can write a mathematical equation relating the force (F), the mass (m), and the radius (r) with the orbital speed (v) based on your data and observations. How can two satellites of different masses remain in the same orbit?

DEMONSTRATING SATELLITE ORBITS

Let's build an apparatus to demonstrate why satellites and spaceships remain in orbit. We will then use the apparatus to help solve a problem involving orbital objects.

You will need the following materials and equipment: plastic garbage bag, garbage can, heavy string (about 10 feet (3 m)), baseball, ball bearings or golf balls, cardboard tube from a roll of paper towels.

Cut the plastic bag so that a single thickness of plastic fits over the top of the garbage can. Stretch the plastic tightly over the top of the garbage can and tie the string all the way around and near the top of the can to hold the plastic tightly.

Place the baseball near the center of the plastic sheet. What happens to the plastic sheet? Place a marble near the edge. This represents a "satellite" in orbit about a planet. What happens is similar to what happens when a nonmoving object is dropped high above the earth.

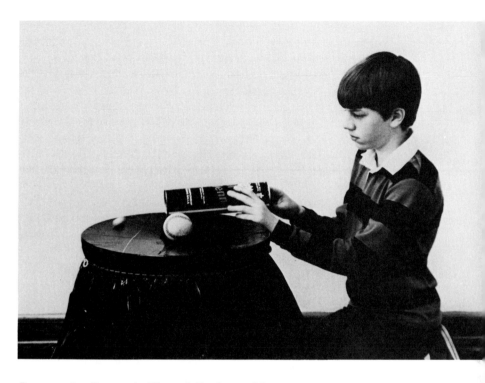

Demonstrating satellite orbits: launching a marble to demonstrate orbital motion.

Now, launch the satellite into "orbit" by raising the cardboard tube up slightly and letting the marble roll down the inside of the tube to gain speed. Observe the path of the "satellite" closely.

By trial and error, see if you can determine what elevation is needed on the cardboard tube to have the marble establish a circular orbit. What happens if the velocity of the marble is too great? Too small? Try aiming the marble at various angles relative to the edge of the garbage can. What happens to the marble when it is launched toward the ball in the middle? Try to aim the marble so that it will stay in "orbit" for the longest time.

According to a physical law first stated by the German scientist Johannes Kepler (1571–1630), the orbit of any planet around the sun is elliptical. This law is called Kepler's first law. A circle is a special case of an ellipse. How did you produce a circular orbit in the above experiment? Using the apparatus, now determine what conditions will produce a noncircular orbit.

One problem faced by space scientists is adjusting orbits to higher or lower altitudes. Often one orbital vehicle needs to rendezvous with another object in another orbit. This can be done by changing the orbital velocity, but as you have seen, this also changes the shape of the orbit.

Here is a problem for which you can use the apparatus you have built. Establish a height for the cardboard tube that will consistently produce a circular orbit. Trace this orbit on the plastic sheet.

How can you leave this orbit and later intersect with it? With a little practice you should be able to create an orbit that intersects with any desired point on the circular orbit. Good luck!

MEASURING MASS IN ORBIT

As space stations are established in orbit about the earth and experiments are performed on these stations, there will be a need to measure the mass of materials for experiments and research. The United States is planning to launch a space station in the 1990s. In space, however, it is impossible to measure mass on a conventional balance. This is because such balances compare the pull of gravity on a known mass with the pull of gravity on an unknown mass. Mass so measured is known as *gravitational mass.* In orbit, the balance and the masses are in free fall and gravity is essentially zero. The balance won't work because the known mass—whatever quantity—will now measure zero.

Fortunately there is a way to measure mass in zero gravity, with a device called an *inertial balance.* An inertial balance measures the mass of an object by how strongly it resists a change in direction or velocity. This property of matter is called *inertia.* Mass measured this

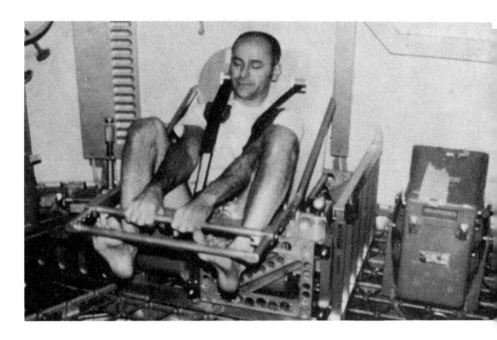

Astronaut Allan L. Bean using an inertial balance to determine his mass. This device, used aboard Skylab, determined the astronaut's mass by timing the oscillations of the spring-loaded platform on which he was sitting.

way is known as *inertial mass.* An object with a lot of inertia is hard to push, for example.

In this project, you will construct and calibrate an inertial balance. You will then attempt to determine whether inertial mass and gravitational mass are the same. If they are, then inertial balances can be used in spacecraft and the results compared with results obtained on earth.

You will need the following materials and equipment: thin metal strip about 3 feet by 1 inch by 1/16 inch (1 m × 3 cm × 2 millimeters, or mm) (a metal ruler works well), metal clamp, masking tape, twenty pennies, stopwatch accurate to the nearest 0.01 second, ten nickels, ten

Measuring mass in orbit: timing the swings of the inertial balance. Note how the ruler is attached to the table.

dimes, laboratory balance accurate to the nearest 0.01 gram, or g.

Attach the metal strip or ruler to a shelf with the clamp. Attach about 2 feet (70 cm) of masking tape to the end of the metal strip, which will be used as a coin holder. Make sure no tape is added or subtracted during all measurements.

Attach ten pennies to the end of the ruler with the tape. Pull the end of the ruler back and let it vibrate at its own natural frequency. Record the time it takes the ruler to make a total of twenty swings. Repeat so that you have a total of three trials. Find the average of the three trials.

Attach ten more pennies for a total of twenty to the end of the ruler. Pull the end of the ruler and let it vibrate as before. Does the greater mass swing faster or slower than the lighter mass? What does this say about the inertia of the larger mass? Repeat so that you have a total of three trials. Find the average of the three trials.

Remove the pennies and tape the ten nickels to the end of the ruler. Record the time for twenty swings. Do three trials as before and find the average. Then remove the nickels and tape the ten dimes to the end of the ruler. Record the time for twenty swings and three trials as before and find the average.

You can use a computer to perform the calculations. Appendix One lists three programs. Program 1 will determine the mass of the ruler and tape from the data collected. Program 2 will calculate the mass of nickels in penny units and the ratio of the mass of one nickel to the mass of one penny. Program 3 will calculate the mass of dimes in penny units and the ratio of the mass of one dime to the mass of one penny.

On a conventional gravitational balance, weigh each type of coin. Calculate the ratio of the mass of a penny to the mass of a nickel. How does this ratio of gravitational masses compare to the inertial mass ratio obtained before? You can repeat the whole experiment using dimes, quarters, or other small objects.

What is the relationship between gravitational mass

and inertial mass? Can an inertial balance be used to determine the mass of objects in orbit? Could an inertial balance be used on the moon, where gravity is one-sixth that on earth? Why don't we use inertial balances on the earth? Do you now understand better the relationship between mass and weight? Can an object have mass but no weight in a weightless environment?

ENERGY STORAGE AND CONVERSION

A major concern for any orbital vehicle is how to power its engines and equipment, especially on a long trip. Once a satellite or space vehicle is in space, data must be transmitted back to earth by radio, computers must operate, cameras click, and so on. All this requires electrical power.

Batteries and fuel cells can serve the purpose for a short period of time, but solar cells are needed when energy requirements extend over any considerable length of time. In direct sunlight, solar cells can supply electrical needs directly and can recharge *secondary cells.* A secondary cell can change electrical energy into chemical energy on charging, then change the chemical energy back to electrical energy while discharging. NASA (the National Aeronautics and Space Administration) expects to power its first space station with a very large solar array (many rows and columns of cells).

Investigating solar energy is an extremely important task for scientists and engineers involved in the space program (and also in research on earthbound energy problems). However, solar-energy experiments are always fun to do, so you shouldn't find the following one much of a task.

You will be converting sunlight into electrical energy, storing the electrical energy in the form of chemical energy, then converting the chemical energy back to electrical energy. You will do this in three distinct steps.

NOTE: SINCE THIS PROJECT INVOLVES USING SOME HAZARDOUS CHEMICALS, YOU SHOULD DO IT UNDER

The four "blades" on this Mariner Mars space
vehicle are actually panels of solar cells, which
convert sunlight to electricity.

SUPERVISION OF YOUR SCIENCE TEACHER AND WHERE YOU HAVE PLENTY OF ROOM TO WORK. MAKE SURE YOU ARE WEARING SAFETY GOGGLES OR A FACE SHIELD.

You will need the following materials and equipment: two AA nickel-cadmium cells, penlight flashlight, 3 feet (1 m) of connecting wire, four 0.42-volt solar batteries, voltmeter (capable of measuring 0.1 volt), AA battery holder, electrolysis apparatus, dilute sulfuric acid (H_2SO_4), copper screen, 1 foot (15 cm) of fine copper wire, 25-by-200-mm test tube with bottom removed, concentrated (30%) potassium hydroxide solution (KOH), filter paper, two #4 two-hole rubber stoppers, 6-mm glass tubing, rubber tubing.

CONVERTING SOLAR ENERGY
TO CHEMICAL ENERGY

Discharge the nickel-cadmium cells completely by putting them into a flashlight and leaving it on until the cells go completely dead.

Connect the four solar batteries in series, with the plus end of one battery connected to the minus end of another battery. Measure the voltage from the solar batteries in direct sunlight. Remember to record all data in your notebook.

Connect the solar cells to one of the nickel-cadmium cells in a battery holder. Measure the voltage across the nickel-cadmium cell while it is charging. Record how many hours it takes for the voltage of the cell to reach 1.4 volts, indicating the cell is fully charged. Experiment with methods of decreasing the time it takes to charge the batteries.

ELECTRICAL ENERGY
TO CHEMICAL ENERGY

Connect your charged nickel-cadmium cells to the electrolysis apparatus filled with dilute sulfuric acid. **HANDLE THE ACID WITH GREAT CARE. WIPE UP ANY SPILLS.** Bubbles will form at each of the electrodes. One of the gases is hydrogen; the other, oxygen. How can you determine which is which?

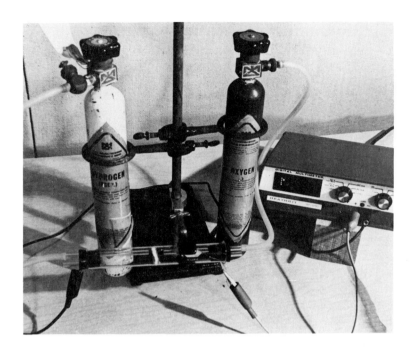

The hydrogen-oxygen fuel cell described in project. In this example, compressed gases are being used to supply the hydrogen and oxygen.

CHEMICAL ENERGY
TO ELECTRICAL
Construct a hydrogen-oxygen fuel cell. Cut two 25-mm-diameter circular electrodes from the copper screen. Cut some thick filter paper into circles 25 mm in diameter. Connect some fine copper wire to the copper electrodes.

Make a "sandwich" of a copper electrode, two pieces of filter paper in the middle, then another copper electrode. Insert the sandwich into the center of the test tube. Soak the filter paper by pouring some of the potassium hydroxide solution into one of the ends of the test tube. Pour off the excess. **BE CAREFUL NOT TO GET THIS SOLUTION ON YOUR HANDS SINCE IT IS CAUSTIC.**

Carefully insert the rubber stoppers containing two glass tubes into each end of the test tube. Make certain the copper wires come out of each end of the test tube and are held in place with the stoppers. Use rubber tubes to transfer the hydrogen and oxygen from the electrolysis apparatus to the fuel cell.

Connect the voltmeter to the fuel cell. The positive lead on the voltmeter should be connected to the wire leading to the oxygen electrode; and the negative lead, to the hydrogen electrode.

Open the valves on the electrolysis apparatus and allow the hydrogen and oxygen to flow slowly through the fuel cell. Any voltmeter reading above 0.0 volts should be considered a success. The authors obtained a voltage of 0.1 volt with the apparatus described here. If no voltage is obtained, try using a digital voltmeter. The efficiency of the electrodes can be improved by covering the copper with platinum. This can be done by dipping the clean electrodes into a solution of platinic chloride for a few minutes. However, platinic chloride is very expensive.

Many other projects can be done with solar cells. Look in the bibliography at the back of this book for the titles of some books that contain such projects.

3

CONDITIONS
IN SPACE

Weightlessness is only one of the unique conditions that must be considered when designing experiments to be performed in space or when planning manned space missions.

For one thing, space is an almost perfect vacuum. Humans cannot venture forth into space without carrying their own air supply or relying on their ship for air, much like a diver. Objects, large or small, encounter no air resistance while moving in space.

At orbital distances from earth, the earth's magnetic field, though still present, is weaker. In deep space, the field may be nonexistent. Navigation by compass is therefore impossible.

The temperature extremes can be huge, depending on which side of the vehicle or satellite is facing the sun and whether the moon or earth is casting a shadow on the spacecraft. Spacecraft are also exposed to streams of solar particles, cosmic rays, and other *electromagnetic radiation.* Electromagnetic radiation includes radio waves, visible light, ultraviolet light, and X-rays.

Other hazards are meteors and dust. The temperature extremes, radiation, meteors and dust, vacuum, and weak magnetic fields—all are of intense interest to scientists and engineers. There is still much to learn about many of these phenomena. They pose a challenge to the scientists and engineers responsible for planning safe and productive space missions. And they offer unimaginable opportunities to those who seek to exploit space for commercial benefit.

REMINDER: MAKE SURE YOU WEAR YOUR SAFETY GOGGLES FOR ALL THE EXPERIMENTS IN THIS CHAPTER.

UNDER PRESSURE

On the surface of the earth, we are swimming in an ocean of air. Air is composed of molecules of various gases, primarily nitrogen, oxygen, and carbon dioxide. As one leaves the surface of the earth, the *density*—the mass per unit volume—of air decreases. At orbital altitudes, the density of gas molecules is so low that a virtual vacuum exists. In deep space, the density is even less! Space is called space for exactly this reason: it is mostly empty.

The normal cabin pressure in a spacecraft such as the space shuttle is the same as it is at the surface of the earth, about 14.7 pounds of force per square inch (1 atmosphere) of surface. However, it may vary from 8 pounds per square inch (PSI) (0.5 atmosphere) to 18.1 PSI (1.3 atmospheres). The pressure outside a spacecraft at an orbital altitude of 200 miles (320 km) is essentially zero. The pressure difference between the inside of the spacecraft and the surrounding space causes a tremendous amount of outward force on the ship's hull. The structural support of the ship must be sufficient to withstand this force or the spacecraft will explode.

To understand the potential force exerted by air pressure, try the following experiment.

You will need the following materials and equipment: 1-gallon metal can with a screw top cover, heat source such as a hot plate or burner, towel.

Make sure the can is empty. Flush it several times with water. The last time you flush the can, leave a small amount of water in the bottom—about ¼ inch (0.5 cm).

With the cap removed, place the can over the heat source. Heat the can until steam comes out of the top of it for about a minute. Using the towel to protect your hands, remove the can from the heat and screw the cap on tight. Set the can on a surface that will not be damaged by the hot can and observe the can. Do you see now the challenge engineers face in trying to design strong, lightweight hulls for spacecraft?

You can design and test some mock spaceships of your own to better understand this challenge. You should be able to get a better idea of the shapes and materials that work best.

You will need the following materials and equipment: aluminum foil, glue, rubber tire patches, an inflation needle, and a tire pump with attached gauge.

It would be difficult to make a spherical spaceship from aluminum foil, but you should be able to make some model spaceships in the shape of a tetrahedron, a cube, a cylinder, or a rectangular solid. (You can make a tetrahedron by gluing together four equilateral triangles.) Find out which of these suggested shapes seems to best stand the pressure.

Since the force on a spaceship in a vacuum is outward, you can test how well your spaceships stand the pressure by inflating them like a basketball.

Glue a rubber tire patch to one of the sides of the spaceship. Use the pump and needle to force air through a hole in the patch into the ship until a leak occurs. Notice any deformation of the ship and the exact pressure when the leak develops.

A spaceship must be as light as possible: getting a ship into orbit is costly, and the cost is proportional to the weight of the ship and the payload.

Using aluminum foil of different thicknesses, find out the optimum ratio of weight of aluminum foil to surface area of foil that will stand 14.7 PSI (1 atmosphere). Hint: If the aluminum is too thick, you will have excess metal; overly thin aluminum won't stand the pressure.

After you have built your own ships, consult tables of sheet metal tensile strength and design a ship with the optimal design in terms of weight, thickness, and shape. Compare your designs with the actual designs used by NASA for the space station (see Appendix Three for address to write for NASA information booklet). You can display your ships, calculations, or designs at a science fair or as a class project.

GAS DIFFUSION

One of the hazards of living, working, or just being in a space vehicle is the possibility that all the air in the capsule will leak out into space. The most likely way this could happen is if a rupture developed in the hull of the ship or the ship were punctured by a meteor. On a very long voyage, it is conceivable that the air inside the ship could leak out even in a well-constructed spacecraft. How could this be?

Gases tend to uniformly occupy any space they are in. This is called *diffusion.* The gas molecules are constantly in motion, colliding with one another and colliding with any barrier they confront. If the gas molecules happen to come upon an opening larger than they are, they will pass right through.

Spacecraft are designed to be completely sealed, but gas molecules are very small and small openings in the hull are inevitable.

In this series of experiments, you will identify some of the factors that affect the rate of gas diffusion from a spacecraft. You also will investigate some of the potential problems associated with maintaining a spacecraft environment suitable for human and animal life. **THESE EXPERIMENTS ARE MORE ADVANCED THAN MANY OF THE OTHERS IN THIS BOOK AND REQUIRE THE USE OF HAZARDOUS CHEMICALS. YOU SHOULD WORK UNDER SUPERVISION.**

The Gemini 8 spacecraft after splashdown in 1966. Note the thickness of the door and of the hull. The capsule has to protect its inhabitants and their equipment from heat and cold, radiation, and meteors; prevent the air inside from leaking out; and withstand the stress and heat of reentry along with the impact of landing.

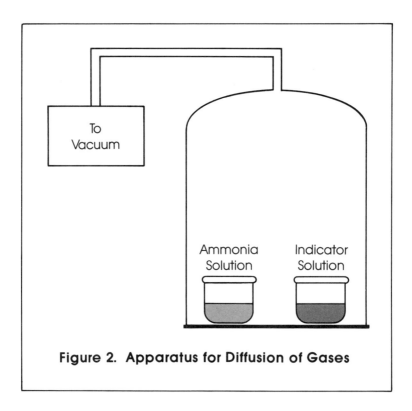

Figure 2. Apparatus for Diffusion of Gases

You will need the following materials and equipment: two small beakers, ammonia solution, ($NH_{3(aq)}$), plastic wrap, rubber band, acid-base indicator phenolpthalein, large bell jar, needle or pin, concentrated hydrogen chloride solution ($HCl_{(aq)}$). You also will need a vacuum pump or other apparatus that can reduce pressure. See Figure 2.

Fill one beaker about one-third full of ammonia solution. **Ammonia has a strong odor, so handle it in a well-ventilated area.** Cover the beaker with some of the plastic wrap and secure it with the rubber band. Fill the other beaker about one-third full of water and add a few drops of phenolpthalein. Place both beakers inside the bell jar or other container that you can evacuate.

Just before you seal the container, poke a hole in the plastic wrap with the needle or pin. Without decreasing the pressure in the jar, observe the beaker with phenolpthalein, which turns pink in a basic solution. When the gaseous ammonia molecules diffuse through the opening, they will come in contact with the phenolpthalein. Ammonia is a base and will turn the indicator pink. Time how long this process takes. Save the pink solution for the next step.

Repeat the above process, only use the concentrated hydrogen chloride solution instead of the ammonia solution in the covered beaker. Hydrogen chloride forms an acid solution, which turns the phenolpthalein solution colorless. Time how long this takes. **TAKE CARE NOT TO GET ANY OF THIS ACID SOLUTION ON YOUR SKIN. IF YOU DO, FLUSH IT WITH WATER IMMEDIATELY.**

The hydrogen chloride molecule is about twice as heavy as the ammonia molecule. How does the speed of the molecules depend on molecular weight?

Repeat the first process with the ammonia at a series of reduced pressures. Be certain the hole size in the plastic is always the same. Use either a vacuum pump or an aspirator to get the reduced pressures. Does the pressure seem to affect how fast the molecules escape?

Repeat the first process with a larger and then a smaller hole in the plastic film. Does the hole size influence how fast the molecules escape?

If you were an astronaut in a spaceship and a tiny meteorite hit your ship and punctured the hull, the air pressure would drop. How fast would it drop? How long would you have to get your space suit on? What are the variables that will control how fast the gas will escape?

Early space flights operated with pure oxygen at reduced cabin pressures to reduce the pressure difference between inside the cabin and outside the ship, and thus the leakage. Find out how a wood splint burns in pure oxygen as compared to air. Then explain why pure oxygen could be dangerous even at low pressure in the event of a cabin fire.

A USEFUL VACUUM

Many useful *compounds*—combinations of the chemical elements—are obtained through a process called *fractional distillation* that involves heating and separating a mixture of compounds. The drawback of this process is that many useful compounds are often destroyed by the heating before they can be isolated. Fractional distillation can be done at low temperatures, saving the chemicals that otherwise might be lost, when the pressure in the distillation chamber is low or nonexistent, as in a vacuum. This is because a substance will boil at lower temperatures as the pressure above or around the liquid is decreased.

On earth, some chemicals are produced by fractional distillation at very low temperatures, but the process is expensive because of the need to build large vacuum or low-pressure chambers. Doing fractional distillation in space might be the solution. Building laboratories in space and transporting the chemicals would obviously be very costly, but in the long run the costs and other benefits might be worth the effort.

In this project, you will learn something about fractional distillation at low temperatures. You will separate an alchohol-and-water mixture at a temperature below the normal boiling point of alcohol. This will serve as an example of how to separate many substances at low temperatures.

You will need the following materials and equipment: tap water, heat source, beaker, thermometer, ethyl alcohol (C_2H_5OH), bell jar or dome, vacuum apparatus with a pressure gauge, graph paper.

Determine the boiling point of water by heating some in a beaker until it just begins to boil. Note the temperature. Repeat this with the alcohol. **USE CAUTION AS THE ALCOHOL IS FLAMMABLE. DO NOT EXPOSE THE VAPORS TO AN OPEN FLAME.**

Pour some tap water at room temperature into the beaker. Place the thermometer into the water. Place the beaker of water in the bell jar or dome. Evacuate the dome with the vacuum pump. Note the exact temperature and pressure at which the water boils. Try this again with slightly warmer water. Repeat the trial so that you have a total of about five different temperatures up to 122°F (50°C) and the corresponding pressures. Construct a graph of your temperature and pressure readings for water and draw a smooth curve through the points.

Repeat the procedure for ethyl alcohol and construct a similar graph. Study both graphs. Select a combination of temperature and pressure that would allow you to boil off the alcohol but not the water. In this way the alcohol can be separated from the mixture with water. Now make a mixture of half water and half alcohol. Using the knowledge you have gained, try to remove the alcohol from the water at a temperature below 122°F (50°C).

In the above project, you simply removed the alcohol. If you wanted to recover the alcohol, how would the apparatus be different? How is this apparatus similar to an apparatus that would use the vacuum of space?

MAGNETISM IN SPACE

The magnetic field of the earth extends into space. Although greatly diminished at orbital altitudes, the field still can affect orbiting vehicles.

Large electrical devices used in space may possess strong magnetic properties. For example, a linear accelerator, a device used to move subatomic particles at great speeds, requires a large magnetic field. Such a device may force an orbiting vehicle to orient with the earth's magnetic field. Large direct-current motors may produce the same effect. It is therefore extremely important for space scientists to understand the earth's magnetic field as it extends into space.

Early scientists visualized the earth's magnetic field as caused by a large bar magnet embedded inside the core of the earth. We now know that the *geomagnetic field*—another name for the earth's magnetic field—is

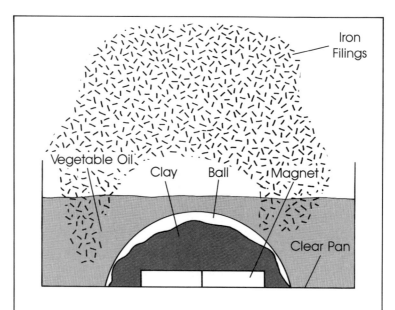

Figure 3. Model of the Earth's Magnetic Field (Cross Sectional View)

caused by the rotation of the earth's molten outer core. However, the bar magnet model (see Figure 3) is still useful for some purposes. The part of space into which the earth's magnetic field extends is called the *magnetosphere*.

In this project you will construct a three-dimensional model of the earth's magnetosphere.

You will need the following materials and equipment: hollow rubber ball, modeling clay, bar magnet small enough to fit inside the rubber ball, clear plastic or glass pan, vegetable oil, iron filings, about 50 feet (15.3 m) of 20-gauge copper wire, 6-volt dry cell, camera (optional).

Cut the ball in half. Fill one-half of the ball with clay. Press the magnet into the clay. Place the half ball, flat side down, in the bottom of the pan. Fill the pan with oil

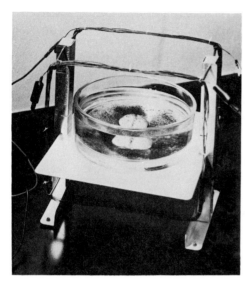

Magnetism-in-space project: electric current flows through the square loops of wire. Adjusting the current can produce a magnetic field to cancel the Earth's field.

until the level of the oil is well above the top of the ball.

Slowly sprinkle the iron filings into the pan. Allow them to fall directly over the ball. Notice how the filings arrange themselves. The curved pattern that you observe is a map of the field lines of the magnetic field of the bar magnet. The earth's magnetosphere is similar. Free-floating magnetic objects within the magnetosphere will align themselves along the field lines. So will a spacecraft that has magnetic properties.

It is possible to cancel out the earth's magnetic field with proper arrangement of some coils of wire carrying an electric current.

Construct two coils of wire with about ten turns on each about the size of the pan containing the magnetosphere model. Place the coils at each pole of the magnetic field of the model earth. Connect one end of one of the coils to a 6-volt dry cell battery. Connect one end of the other coil to the other pole of the battery. Complete the circuit by connecting the two remaining wire ends.

Observe the effect of the electrical coils on the magnetosphere model. Reverse the direction of the current flow in the coils by switching the wires at the battery. Is the effect the same? Scientists believe that coils like this aboard a spacecraft may be used to cancel out magnetic fields created on the spacecraft so that it will not tumble end over end.

Another approach to solving this problem is to use an identical magnet to cancel out the magnetic field. Try different orientations of a second bar magnet. If a second magnet is brought near the model perpendicular to the model's field, how is the field disturbed? What if the magnet is brought parallel to the model's field?

You could photograph how the iron filings are changed when another bar magnet is brought near the model in order to have a permanent record of the effects.

OBSERVING SOLAR ACTIVITY

Sunspots and solar flares are caused by disturbances on the surface of the sun that send out streams of electrically charged particles. These can affect radio communications on earth and also between space vehicles and earth stations. Because space vehicles need to maintain radio contact with earth (some satellites and spacecraft can be controlled from earth), understanding and being able to predict sunspot activity is extremely important. Further, solar flares put out intense amounts of radiation that may directly cause harm to astronauts.

In this project, you will explore the effects of sunspot activity on various terrestrial phenomena.

You will need the following materials and equipment: telescope, two pieces of cardboard about 2 feet by 2 feet (70 cm × 70 cm), knife or scissors, marking pen, camera, AM radio, short-wave receiver.

Set up the telescope in an open area. This project must be done on a clear, sunny day. Point the telescope toward the sun, but **DO NOT LOOK INTO THE TELESCOPE! DIRECT SUNLIGHT CAN SERIOUSLY DAMAGE YOUR EYES.**

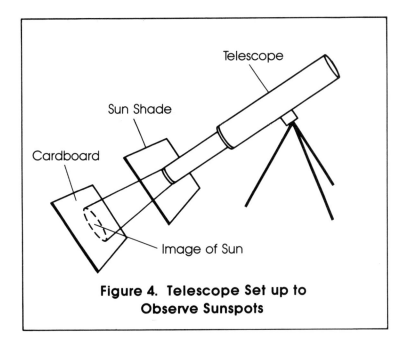

Figure 4. Telescope Set up to Observe Sunspots

AT NO TIME DURING THE OBSERVATIONS SHOULD YOU LOOK DIRECTLY AT THE SUN.

Cut a hole in one piece of cardboard so that it will fit over the smaller end of the telescope. This will act as a sunshade. Hold the cardboard below the eyepiece of the telescope (see Figure 4). Focus the telescope and vary the distance of the cardboard until you obtain a sharp image of the sun on the cardboard.

Study the image carefully. You should be able to see some dark patches that usually occur in pairs of different-sized spots. These are sunspots. With the marking pen, outline the circle illuminated on the cardboard and then mark the position of each sunspot.

Repeat this procedure at regular intervals of either a day or a week. Construct a graph of the number of sunspots versus the number of days. Do the sunspots change? Are there always the same number of them? Do the sunspots move? Is there a pattern to sunspot activi-

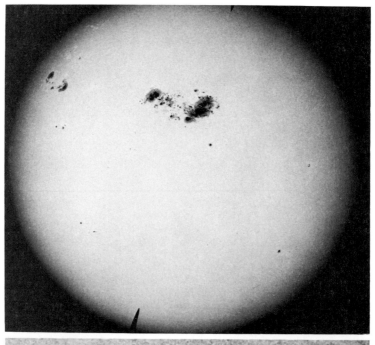

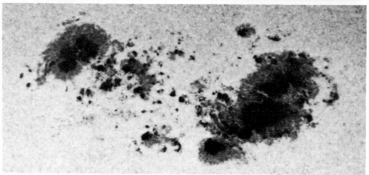

Top: *photograph of sun showing sunspots.*
Bottom: *enlargement of sunspots. Note similarity between patterns around the darker part of the spots and the patterns formed by iron filings around a magnet. Can you find out why they're similar?*
Facing page: *solar prominences are active in the vicinity of sunspots. They can be seen during solar eclipses.*

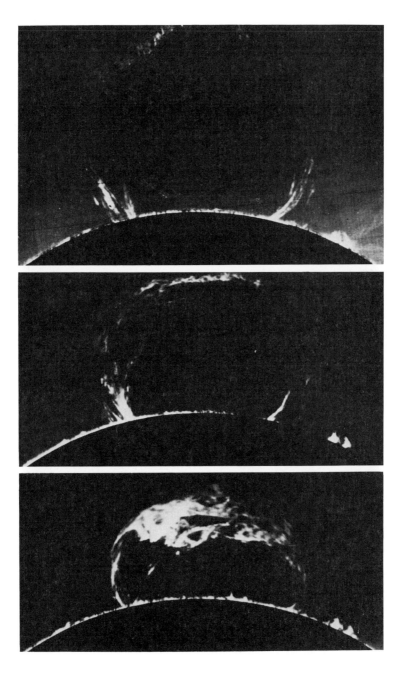

ty? The study of sunspots can be a long-term project since the number of sunspots changes over a period of many years.

Once you have completed these preliminary investigations, you are ready to try one or more of the following projects.

1. Photograph the sunspots you observe and—**ON THE CARDBOARD, NOT THROUGH THE TELESCOPE**—determine their pattern of movement across the face of the sun.

2. From time to time, you hear in the news that communications are disrupted here on earth. What are the sunspots doing when this occurs?

3. Construct a calendar showing when space missions would be safe from solar radiation that may result from high sunspot activity.

4. Does sunspot activity affect the distance that radio signals can be transmitted from one point on the earth to another? Keep a careful record of what AM radio stations you hear at night, their distance, and how clear their signals are.

5. Can you correlate sunspot activity with the "Geo-alerts" broadcast by government station WWV in Fort Collins, Colorado, on a frequency of 2.5, 5, 10, 15, and 20 megahertz on a short-wave receiver?

6. Find out if there is any connection between sunspot activity and auroras. To be able to observe auroras, you will have to be living in the extreme northern United States or in Canada.

7. Does extreme solar activity interact with the earth's magnetic field to a point that compasses are affected?

8. Do sunspots affect weather patterns? Droughts?

SPACESHIPS, HOT AND COLD

As pointed out in the beginning of this chapter, vehicles in space are subjected to extreme differences in temperature. A spaceship in direct sunlight absorbs energy and can become quite hot, while when shaded from direct sunlight it can become very cold. These extremes can cause the interior of a spacecraft to get dangerously hot or cold. The temperature differences from one part of the spacecraft to another can also cause stress in the structure of the hull.

This project gives you a chance to learn how various surfaces absorb energy (in this case, light energy). We will then try to use the knowledge obtained to control the temperature inside a model spacecraft.

You will need the following materials and equipment: food cans such as 1-pound coffee cans, white paint, black paint, tape, two thermometers, 100-watt light bulb, light bulb holder. Other materials and paint may also be used as you experiment with the absorbing properties of various surfaces.

Cover one of two identical cans with white paint and the other with black paint. Puncture holes just slightly larger than your thermometer diameter in the bottom of each can. Place the cans bottom side up equidistant from the light bulb, as shown in Figure 5. Put some tape around each thermometer so that each thermometer projects an equal distance into the can.

Hook up and turn on the light bulb. Record the maximum temperature reached on each thermometer. What surface color seems to be the best absorber of light from the bulb? Other surface materials such as black or white cloth, paper, plastic of various colors, aluminum foil, and paint of different colors could be used on the cans. You also can experiment with different surface textures.

If you have an Apple II computer and a special device called a thermistor (a device used to detect temperature change), turn to Appendix One, which contains a program (#4) you can use to measure temperature and plot the changing temperature with time. In this way you could have a permanent record of how each sur-

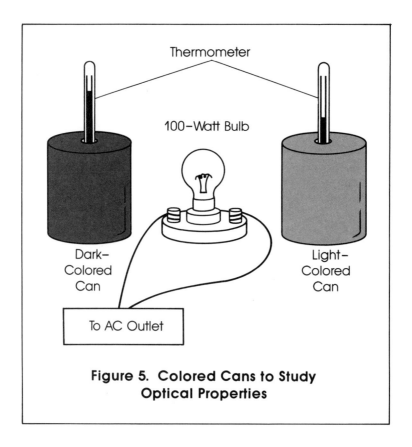

Figure 5. Colored Cans to Study Optical Properties

face responds to the light. Appendix Three lists a few sources of thermistors.

Remove both the top and bottom from one of the cans. Cover the left half of the can with white paint and the right half with black paint. Place the light bulb in the center of the can. Position each of the two thermometers on the outside of the can the same distance from the can, one from the white surface and one from the black surface.

Turn on the bulb and observe the maximum temperature reached by each thermometer. Experiment with a variety of other materials as well as smooth or rough surfaces. For example, mix some sand into the paint before you cover the can.

Apparatus for testing thermal radiation from various surfaces in the project titled Spaceships, Hot and Cold

Try to come up with a system that will maintain a temperature inside a can between 55°F (13°C) and 95°F (35°C) with the light bulb outside of the can. This is the normal temperature range inside a spacecraft such as the space shuttle. Try a combination of surfaces that will maintain this temperature under a variety of light conditions. If this becomes difficult, devise a method of radiating the excess heat. Try experimenting with the shape and orientation of the can.

4

PRINCIPLES OF
MATERIALS SCIENCE

The space program has provided many materials that have already become an integral part of our lives, for example, high-temperature ceramics for cooking, Velcro fasteners, "space blankets" made of Mylar, plastics, and semiconductor components. What new materials will the laboratory of space provide us in the future? The answer depends on what characteristics of the space environment materials scientists can exploit. *Materials science* is the application of science principles to the investigation of the relationships between the structure and properties of materials.

The following projects enable you to investigate some of the processes of materials science that are used by space scientists.

ARE YOUR WEARING YOUR SAFETY GOGGLES OR A FACE SHIELD? IF NOT, PUT IT ON BEFORE BEGINNING ANY OF THE PROJECTS IN THIS CHAPTER.

CONVECTION

Convection in fluids is the movement due to density differences within the fluid. Density differences cause significant convection only in the presence of gravity.

A comparison of crystals grown on earth (left) and on Skylab (right). The space-grown crystals have better-defined edges and smoother facets. They also more clearly display the typical crystal structure of this substance.

Convection plays a role in the formation of crystals. When certain crystals are growing, they produce heat, which then causes convection currents in and around the growing crystals. These currents disturb the crystal growth, mixing impurities in with the crystal and creating flaws in the crystal's structure.

When crystals are grown in zero gravity, on the other hand, convection currents are eliminated. Several large silicon crystals high in purity and low in defects have already been produced on Skylab. In the future, some types of crystals may be manufactured in quantity in space.

The purpose of this project is to determine the characteristics and causes of convection currents in the normal-gravity—*one-G*—environment of earth.

You will need the following materials and equipment: 1- to 2-liter Pyrex beaker, crystals of a colored salt such as potassium permanganate ($KMnO_4$) or copper(II) sulfate ($Cu(SO_4)_2$), hot plate or lab burner, camera (optional), plastic model glue, about 12 inches (30 cm) of thread.

Fill the beaker with water. Put a few coarse crystals of the colored salt on the bottom of the beaker and heat very gently. What do you observe? You might want to photograph the action for further study.

Make a diagram of the direction of current flow relative to the direction of gravity. Form a hypothesis as to what causes the flow in the beaker. How could you test this hypothesis in a way other than by heating the liquid?

Refill the beaker with room-temperature water. Glue a large salt crystal to a piece of thread. Suspend the crystal in the beaker of water. Observe the area around the crystal carefully. There is little or no temperature difference in the beaker, so if currents are observed, what is causing them? Allow the beaker to stand undisturbed for about an hour. Can you detect any evidence of currents in the beaker after this period of time?

In both of the above cases, convection currents were in evidence. What common factor in each was responsible for the convection? What would happen if you heated the water while the crystal was dissolving in it?

BUOYANCY AND SEDIMENTATION

Any substance, whether a particle of a solid, a drop of a liquid, or even a gas bubble immersed in a fluid, is always subjected to a *buoyant force* by the fluid. This force lifts a substance against gravity so that there is less net gravitational pull on the object. The net force may be upward or downward depending on the difference in densities of the substances.

*Many important experiments to find out
the effects of space on materials, processes,
and organisms were conducted on Skylab.*

In one-G, it is possible to keep only very small particles suspended for a long time. Very large particles whose density is greater than that of the fluid will settle out in a process called *sedimentation*.

Experiments done on Skylab have shown that temporary *suspensions* produced in a one-G environment would result in an almost permanent suspension if done in a zero-gravity condition. A suspension results when a substance is mixed with but remains undissolved in a fluid or solid. This could be an advantage if you wished to make a uniform suspension of two materials that did not mix.

For example, two metals that ordinarily would not form an *alloy* could be melted together in zero gravity and thoroughly mixed, then allowed to cool to form a solid. An alloy is a mixture of two metals melted together. The solid that results could not be produced in a one-gravity environment because of the buoyant effects of metals on each other. On the other hand, the absence of buoyancy and sedimentation can be a problem in zero gravity if you wish to separate two substances by sedimentation.

In the following projects, you will observe the phenomena of buoyancy and sedimentation and learn what causes these effects. Then we will consider and investigate the effects of the absence of gravity on buoyancy and sedimentation.

You will need the following materials and equipment: small bottle with removable screw cap, water, cooking oil, about 6 feet (2 m) of cord, dry-cleaning fluid, fine sand or mud, sawdust or cork bits, centrifuge.

BUOYANCY EFFECTS

Fill the bottle nearly full with water. Shake the bottle vigorously so that small bubbles of air become suspended. Note the milky appearance of the water while the air is suspended. What happens to the air bubbles? Why? If gravity were absent, what do you think would happen?

Put a small quantity of cooking oil in the water and shake the bottle vigorously. Observe the actions of the oil and water. Can you explain why the oil droplets behave the way they do? Pay particular attention to the interface between the two liquids. Turn the bottle upside down. What happens?

While keeping the bottle inverted, tie the cord around the neck of the bottle. Shake the bottle again to disperse the oil. Then swing the bottle around in a circle for about ten seconds. Stop and observe the oil and water. Did they separate as before? If so, was it faster or slower?

Empty the bottle and add clean water. Add a small

quantity of dry-cleaning fluid to the water. Repeat the same procedures that you did with the oil and water. Form a hypothesis as to why the cleaning fluid behaves differently than the oil. Try to test this with further experiments.

SEDIMENTATION EFFECTS
Place a small sample of sand or mud into the container of water. Shake the container so that the sand or mud and water are mixed thoroughly, and observe the solid particles. If settling occurs, do all of the particles settle at the same rate?

Find out if your school has a centrifuge for separating insoluble substances from solutions and ask if you can use it on your soil sample. What effect does the centrifuge have on your suspension? How do you think the suspension of sand would behave in zero gravity?

Place a small sample of sawdust or bits of cork in a bottle nearly filled with water. Shake and observe the mixture. Can you explain why some of the wood particles move to the water surface faster than others? Try the centrifuge on this suspension, too. Will particles float on water like this in zero gravity?

Do your observations of sedimentation support or refute your hypothesis for the causes of the separation of liquids in the previous experiment?

HYDROSTATIC PRESSURE

Fluids are substances that can flow. Liquids and gases both are types of fluids. A liquid such as water that occupies a tall beaker or glass jar exerts a force on every part of the area of the sides and bottom of the vessel. This is called *hydrostatic pressure.*

Hydrostatic pressure plays an important role in the functioning of your body, and of many machines and scientific instruments. It is therefore important to understand how the lack of gravity affects the hydrostatic pressure of fluids.

In this project, you will simulate a weightless environment for a short period of time and observe the behavior of fluids in it.

You will need the following materials and equipment: empty coffee can, metal punch, video camera (optional), old plastic beach ball or substitute, old garden hose, inflation needle used to inflate a basketball, tape, hose clamp.

Puncture some holes in various places on the side of the can with the metal punch. Be sure to put a hole near the top of the can and one near the bottom. Fill the can with water and observe the streams of water coming from the holes. Note any ways the streams differ. Why do they differ? Does one particular stream change as the can empties? Why?

Now, find a place where you can drop the can from a height of at least 10 to 15 feet (3–5 m). Fill the can with water and be prepared to observe the streams of water while it is falling. If you have a video camera, videotape the falling can for later study. Objects in *free fall*, the unhindered fall through air, experience near zero gravity just like in space.

Now, drop the leaking can. What happens to the streams of water coming from the can? Form a hypothesis that explains the cause of hydrostatic pressure. You can test that hypothesis in the following similar situation.

Now, puncture the beach ball with equal-sized holes in various places around the ball. Cut the old garden hose about 10 feet (3 m) from the end that attaches to the faucet. Attach the inflation needle to the hose with the hose clamp. You may need to build up the needle base with tape so that a proper seal is formed. Attach the hose to the faucet and force water into the ball through the needle. Compare the results of this experiment with those of the previous one.

Predict what will happen if you drop the ball as you did the can. Now try it! Do you think hydrostatic pressure exists in space?

A liquid bridging the gap across two surfaces.
Rotation of the liquid causes the asymmetrical shape.
The liquid is held in place by surface tension.
This photograph was taken on Skylab.

SURFACE TENSION

Surface tension is caused by molecules of a liquid that tend to attract one another. This attraction causes a resistive force on the surface of a liquid similar to that caused by a rubber balloon stretched over the mouth of a jar but much, much weaker. Surface tension effects can be—and have been—used to great advantage in space, for example, to grow very pure silicon crystals. Liquids can be contained in a *floating zone* by surface tension. In zero-G, this floating zone is much larger and can be used to remove impurities from crystals. Much larger crystals can be grown in space than on earth because the surface tension effects are not masked by gravity-induced effects.

In this project, you will observe the effects of surface tension and conduct experiments with methods of reducing surface tension.

Astronaut Joseph Kerwin blowing an air bubble into a liquid. The bubble will go to the center of the liquid in zero-G. This effect, called "bubble centering," is the result of surface tension.

You will need the following materials and equipment: water, large beaker, metal paper clips, liquid dishwashing soap, ethyl alcohol (C_2H_5OH), several glass or plastic capillary tubes of various diameters, shallow baking pan, ground black pepper, ruler, 4-inch (10-cm) wire hoop, needle, commercial bubble solution, thread, plastic bubble pipe, waxed paper.

Fill the beaker with clean water. Using a metal paper clip bent in the shape of an L, carefully lower a second, unbent paper clip onto the surface of the water. What happens? Add a drop of soap to the water. What happens to the paper clip?

Obtain some fresh water. Dip the capillary tubes into various liquids such as water, alcohol, and soapy water and measure the height the liquid inside the tube rises over the liquid surface outside. Does the diameter of the tube influence the height of the liquid in the tube? Do different liquids rise to different heights? Does the material that the capillary tube is made of affect the height the liquid rises? Devise an experiment to test your hypotheses.

Shake pepper all over the surface of the water in a shallow pan so the water is covered. Now add 1 drop of the liquid soap near the center of the water. What happens? Clean the pan and repeat the demonstration, this time dropping the soap near the edge of the pan. Why do the pepper particles move? What is driving them?

Many other interesting projects are possible with soap bubbles. Tie a piece of the thread rather loosely across the metal hoop. Dip the ring into the bubble solution to form a soap bubble film. Puncture the film on one side of the thread with a hot needle and observe how the film on the remaining side pulls on the thread. Form a soap bubble by blowing slowly into the plastic pipe. What happens to the bubble when the pipe is held free in the air? Why do the bubbles always tend to form spheres?

Observe droplets of water on a piece of the waxed paper. What shape is each droplet? How does the shape compare with the shape of the soap bubbles? Touch the droplet with a little liquid soap. Does the droplet change shape? Why or why not?

Phenomena in nature always tend to do that which requires the least energy. With this in mind, form a hypothesis as to why liquids confined by surface tension tend to form the shapes that they do. Test this hypothesis with various bubble-forming apparatus, for example, wire loops and frames, bubble blowers, and pipes.

5

APPLICATIONS OF
MATERIALS SCIENCE

In space we can study and better understand phenomena in materials processing that in turn will allow improvement of processes conducted on earth. In addition, unique materials impossible to form on earth can be manufactured in space, for example, near-perfect crystals, metal alloys and foams, superior structural materials, high-strength composites, high-purity pharmaceuticals, and uniform fiber sheets. Many processes such as combustion and fluid flow occur much differently in space than on earth.

The following projects will allow you to explore the behavior of materials and some of the processes of materials science.

DON'T FORGET YOUR SAFETY GOGGLES!

CRYSTALS

Crystals made of silicon or other materials are essential for semiconductors, computers, radiation sensors, and lasers. These crystals must be very pure and structurally sound in order to function efficiently. Zero gravity permits scientists to grow large, nearly perfect crystals by elimi-

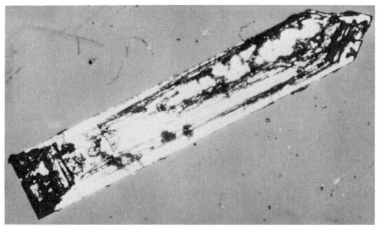

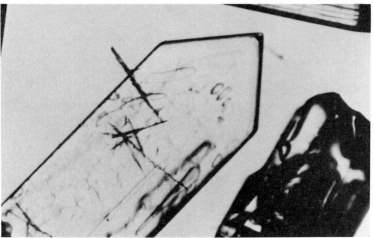

Top: *An earth-grown crystal of urea, an important organic compound found in human waste and used in manufacturing processes. The crystal is several millimeters long and contains flaws.* Bottom: *A space-grown crystal of urea. It is more pure and more perfectly formed than its earth-grown cousin. Scientists are studying the properties of such crystals in hopes of developing new and better products.*

nating convection, buoyancy, and hydrostatic pressure. The weightless environment also enables crystals to be processed without containers. This eliminates deformation and absorption of impurities from the container.

In this project, you will grow crystals in one-G using four different methods of crystallization to investigate the effects of gravity on crystal formation.

You will need the following materials and equipment: 8.0 g of potassium nitrate (KNO_3), two 6-inch (15-cm) test tubes, a 25-milliliter (25-ml) graduated cylinder, thermometer, laboratory balance, heat source (gas burner), magnifying glass, 10.0 g of sodium chloride (NaCl), clean cotton cloth, watch glass, 100-ml beaker, 1.0 g of iodine (I_2), heavy paper, 4.0 g of paradichlorobenzene ($C_6H_4Cl_2$) (solid bathroom deodorant-moth crystals).

1. Obtain some potassium nitrate from your science teacher or from a chemical supply house. Dissolve about 8 g of the chemical in 10 ml of water at 122°F (50°C) in the test tube. Allow this mixture to cool slowly.

Using the magnifying glass, observe the crystals as they form. Note where they form and their shape and size. Where do you think the crystals would form in zero gravity? Why?

2. Dissolve as much sodium chloride as possible in some water in a test tube to produce a saturated solution. Filter the solution through some cloth into the beaker and leave uncovered for several days. Study with the magnifying glass. What shape(s) do you see? Are all the crystals identical? If not, what causes some of the crystals to form imperfectly? How could this be prevented?

3. Obtain about 1 g of solid iodine. **HANDLE THE IODINE CAREFULLY. THE VAPORS ARE POISONOUS. DO THIS PROJECT IN A WELL-VENTILATED AREA AND UNDER ADULT SUPERVISION.**

Place the iodine in the 100-ml beaker and cover with the watch glass. Heat slowly with the burner. Observe the crystal growth on the sides of the beaker and on the watch glass. Do you think the crystals would form differently if this were done in zero gravity? Why? Would this be of advantage to the formation of materials?

4. Heat about 4 g of paradichlorobenzene in a test tube until it just melts. Pour the liquid paradichlorobenzene into a paper cone. When the material is cool, break the cone into pieces and observe. Note any differences in the crystals from the top of the cone to the bottom. Suppose this process were done in zero gravity. How would this change the crystallizing process? Why?

How could zero-G be produced for a short time on earth? Could any of the methods you've used to form crystals be adapted to form crystals in such an environment? Experiment with these methods and try to form larger and more uniform-sized crystals.

ALLOYS

Metallic alloys, technically, are solid solutions of two or more substances. The metals are melted, mixed, then allowed to solidify—a complex process. Even though the metals are thoroughly mixed in the melt, as they begin to solidify, separation occurs between the solid and liquid phases.

In zero gravity, there is neither convection nor hydrostatic pressure, so mixtures of metals insoluble in one another can be made to form a uniform alloy. Some unique materials were prepared on Skylab in the early 1970s. Experiments on Spacelab, the orbiting laboratory flown aboard the space shuttle in 1984, will continue to produce high-strength alloys and prototypes of aircraft turbine blades that consist of a single crystal.

In this project, you will form a low-temperature alloy in one-G and in free fall. **Do this project under adult supervision.** As always in the laboratory, wear safety glasses. **Also wear heavy gloves for this project.**

You will need the following materials and equipment: 5.00 g of bismuth metal (Bi), 2.81 g of lead metal (Pb), 2.19 g of tin metal (Sn), small porcelain crucible, propane torch, tongs to handle the crucible, large container of water (such as a garbage can).

Find the melting point of bismuth, lead, and tin from a reference book or chemistry textbook.

Melt the three metals together in the porcelain crucible with the propane torch. The mixture, known as Rose's metal, is an alloy of the three metals. This alloy is used for automatic sprinkler systems because of its low melting point.

Melt the alloy in some boiling water and observe. Allow the metal to cool and watch the crystals as they form. What shape do you think the metal would form if it were allowed to cool in zero gravity?

Find a place where you can safely drop the liquid metal from a height of about 25 to 40 feet (8–13 m). The third floor of a building or tower with a large open area below would do. Get a large container of water to cushion the landing of the metal pellets. **Again, be careful when selecting a place to perform this project. Make sure the metal will not fall on anyone or anything that may be damaged!**

Heat the metal until it is *just melted!* **DO NOT HEAT THE METAL FURTHER ONCE IT IS MELTED.** Drop small amounts of the metal from the height into the water. Recover the pellets and observe their shape. What shape is the pellet? What shape do you think the pellet would be if it were formed in orbit? Are the crystals in the pellet arranged any differently than the first time you observed them? How? Why?

COMPOSITES

A *composite material,* or simply a composite, is formed when one material is suspended in another material while it solidifies. In space, it is possible to make a variety of composites that would be impossible to make on earth.

One of the reasons is that on earth differences in density cause materials to separate before they harden.

For example, in space it would be possible to suspend metal oxide particles in a metal to produce materials that retain their strength and hardness at high temperature. Let's make a composite material and investigate its properties.

You will need the following materials and equipment: cloth gloves, screw eye, old wooden board, kite string, bathroom scale, rubber gloves, Superglue or similar fast-setting glue.

Determine the breaking strength of the string. Put on the cloth gloves to protect your hands. Screw the screw eye into the board and attach some of the string. Place the bathroom scale on the board, with the screw eye and string near the top of the scale as shown in the photograph on page 70.

Get on the scale and record your exact weight to the nearest pound. Increase the pull steadily on the string until it breaks. Record the weight at that moment.

Put on the rubber gloves. Take another piece of string, and soak it with Superglue. Then hang it up so that it will not curl as it dries. Allow several hours for it to dry. **Be careful not to get the glue on your fingers.**

Now you have a composite. Test its breaking strength as before. Is the breaking strength different from that of the original string?

Test the stiffness of the untreated string by seeing what length will support its own weight without bending. Hold the string so it is just barely sticking out between your thumb and index finger. Pull the string out a short distance and see if it will support its own weight. If it doesn't bend, repeat this step. Record the length that first bends under its own weight. Then compare the stiffness of the treated and untreated strings.

Try to form other composites and test them in a similar way. Try various types of glue or string. Perhaps introduce a third material such as pencil lead shavings or talcum powder. Determine what changes in properties occur.

Method for testing the breaking strength of a string

Try to develop a composite with specific properties such as high strength and high flexibility. Produce your own unique material.

ELECTROPHORESIS AND ION MIGRATION

Electrophoresis is the movement of molecules, cells, or other particles through a fluid under the action of an electric field.

Apparatus that utilize electrophoresis are among the most powerful tools a researcher has to monitor life processes. Such apparatus can separate and detect proteins, which are the very building blocks of life. Recently the process of electrophoresis has been used in space to separate materals in large quantities that can be used to fight diabetes. In 1977, NASA proposed the construction of a space factory, one of whose main purposes would be to produce pharmaceuticals by electrophoresis. A full-scale pharmaceutical laboratory is scheduled to be in orbit by the late 1980s.

On earth, the process of electrophoresis is extremely limited by gravity. Because an electric field is used in electrophoresis, hydrogen and oxygen gases are produced at the two electrodes that generate the electric field. On earth, in one-G, the bubbles rise to the surface of the liquid, disrupting the fluid flow. In zero gravity, the bubbles stay near the electrodes, where they can be drawn off. Another difficulty in one-G is that the electric current heats the carrier solution, causing unwanted convection currents.

Perhaps the most serious problem in one-G is sedimentation. The particles moving through the carrier solution are more dense and tend to sink or settle out. In zero-G, there is no such tendency.

Separating materials in a one-G environment will probably never be as efficient as in space, where in experiments so far, the yields have been increased about four hundred times over what is possible on earth.

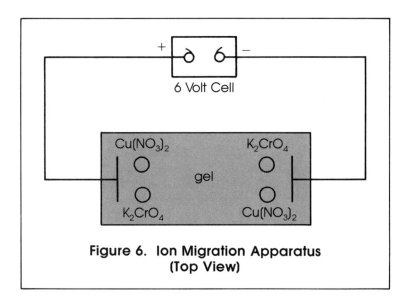

**Figure 6. Ion Migration Apparatus
(Top View)**

Ion migration, the movement of ions in an electric field, is similar to electrophoresis. Charged atoms or molecules—ions—replace the molecules or cells. Studying ion migration can be a useful way to learn about electrophoresis, which is exactly what you will be doing in this project. **Do this project under adult supervision.**

You will need the following materials and equipment: distilled water, 250-ml beaker, heat source, 2.0 g of agar gel, 8.0 g of ammonium nitrate (NH_4NO_3), shallow glass baking dish about 10 inches by 6 inches by 1½ inches (25 cm × 15 cm × 4 cm), 1.88 g of copper(II) nitrate ($Cu(NO_3)_2$), 1.94 g of potassium chromate (K_2CrO_4), empty pill bottle with 1-inch (2.5-cm) opening, two connecting wires, copper metal strips about 1 inch by 4 inches (2 cm × 10 cm), 6-volt lantern battery.

Heat 200 ml of distilled water almost to boiling. Add the 8.0 g of ammonium nitrate and the 2.0 g of agar gel to the water. Boil gently for a few minutes and stir to dissolve the gel. Pour the solution while it is still warm into the shallow glass dish. Allow the gel to set up for several hours before proceeding.

Make a solution of copper(II) nitrate by dissolving 1.88 g of the solid to make a total of 20.0 ml of solution. Make a solution of potassium chromate by dissolving 1.94 g of the solid to make a total of 20.0 ml of solution.

Cut four round holes in the gel about 1 inch (2.5 cm) in diameter with the pill bottle. Fill two of the holes with the copper(II) nitrate solution and the other two holes with potassium chromate solution. See Figure 6.

Attach the wires to the center of the copper strips and put the strips into the gel solution. Connect the other ends of the wires to the battery. It doesn't matter which way the battery is connected. Wait about six hours.

Copper(II) ions have a positive charge and are colored blue. Chromate ions are charged negative and colored yellow.

Do the copper(II) ions move toward one of the electrodes? What about the chromate ions? Explain what is happening in the region where the copper(II) ions meet the chromate ions. Mix a few drops of the two solutions together in a separate beaker. Does the same color form? What causes the color?

Note the pattern of movement through the gel. Try changing the variables in the cell until you get a good understanding of the nature of the migration. Can the speed and direction of the flow be controlled? How? Can you get the ions to flow in the same direction but in different streams? This would closely simulate electrophoresis. How could gravity be used to control the migration?

FLOCCING

Examine several sheets of different kinds of paper by holding them up to a bright light source. The dark regions you observe are called *flocs*. These are caused by an attractive force between the paper fibers that causes them to clump together when they are in a suspension. This is called *floccing*. All fibers, bubbles, or other suspended solids have a tendency to floc to varying degrees.

In papermaking, floccing is undesirable because it leads to nonuniform sheets of paper. Special chemicals can control floccing to some extent, but considerable research still goes into trying to understand and control floccing.

Floccing can be effectively studied in space because gravity does not mask the forces causing the formation of flocs. A student project flown on the space shuttle in late 1985 was designed to determine if the lack of gravity affects the floccing process.

The purpose of this project is to investigate the formation of flocs and to try various methods of controlling floccing.

You will need the following materials and equipment: tissue, water, blender, shallow glass dish, spray laundry starch, cotton balls.

Add a sheet of tissue paper and 400 ml of water to the blender, set on medium speed, and grind the mixture for about 20 seconds. Pour the resulting suspension into the shallow glass dish. What do you observe?

Return the paper fiber slurry to the blender and spray with starch for 3 seconds. Blend for about 5 seconds. Pour the suspension into a shallow dish and carefully observe to see if there is any change in the floccing process. Return the mixture to the blender and add another 3-second burst of starch. Blend as before. Pour the suspension into the dish and observe as before, looking for changes. Does the suspension of starch affect the floccing process?

Try different amounts of starch in order to minimize the amount of floccing. Try different brands or types of starch. Experiment with other fibers, for example: Grind up some cotton balls as you did the tissue. Is the floccing the same? Can you control it with the starch?

COMBUSTION

In this project, you will investigate the nature of burning. You will observe a flame in one-G and also in a zero-G environment.

You will need the following materials and equipment: small wax candle, small can lid, tissue paper, wide-mouth plastic bottle with screw cap, fire extinguisher, stop-watch, movie or video camera (optional).

Examine the candle closely. How is it constructed? Where is the wick located? Light the candle and attach it to the can top with a little of the wax.

Look closely. Can you see the flame melt the wax and then the molten wax flow up the wick? How might this be different in zero gravity?

Look at the flame carefully. Can you notice that it is moving? What causes it to move? Remember that combustion requires heat, fuel, and oxygen. Where does oxygen enter the flame?

Hold a piece of the tissue paper just high enough above the candle so it does not catch fire. Hold the tissue loosely. What happens to the tissue? Why?

Attach the candle to the bottom of the inside of the plastic container with some wax. Be sure the container is clean and contains no flammable material. Do not use glass, or it will break. **BE CAREFUL THAT THE PLASTIC BOTTLE DOES NOT CATCH ON FIRE. KEEP YOUR FIRE EXTINGUISHER HANDY! KEEP THE CANDLE SMALL TO REDUCE THE FIRE HAZARD.**

Light the candle and quickly put the cover on tightly. With the stopwatch, find out exactly how many seconds it takes the candle to go out. Start the stopwatch the moment the cover is placed on the jar. Record the time. Why does the candle eventually go out?

Arrange to have an assistant drop the burning candle in the plastic bottle a vertical distance of about 20 feet (6 m). You could do this in a darkened gymnasium or on a dark, calm night from a piece of playground apparatus. **KEEP THE POSSIBILITY OF FIRE HAZARD IN MIND WHEN PLANNING THE EXPERIMENT.**

From a distance, observe the candle as it falls. You might want to film or videotape this part of the experiment. Record the time it takes for the candle to go out as before.

Were the results the same as the last time? Why did

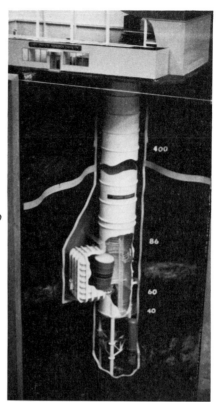

Model of the NASA drop tower used to produce zero-G effect. The container located near the bottom is filled with impact-absorbing material to cushion the landing of the experimental package. When in use, the entire tower is evacuated of all air.

the candle go out this time? How does the burning differ in free fall? Why? Try dropping from different heights or with different-sized containers.

This project demonstrates one way that free fall can be used to simulate zero-G to study a phenomenon for a short period of time. NASA has a facility that can simulate zero-G through free fall for as long as 5 seconds.

Many experiments are tested in this facility to get them ready for space flight.

The orbital environment provides long-duration zero-G conditions. Some day materials scientists will be working in facilities in orbit to improve the quality and quantity of products for use on the earth.

6

PLANTS, ANIMALS, AND MICROORGANISMS

Since the beginning of the space program, scientists have been interested in how space flights and the space environment affect plants and animals. Animals were first used as substitutes for humans by scientists who wanted to prepare humans for space flight. Early animal subjects were mammals with body structures as close to human as possible.

Scientists were most concerned with the effects of launch acceleration, prolonged weightlessness, and reentry forces on the human body. Not until the feasibility of manned space flight was firmly established were plants and animals studied for their own sake, with the first such experiments being performed on Skylab in the 1970s.

BIOLOGICAL CLOCKS

The first Skylab experiments involved the study of *circadian rhythms* in pocket mice and fruit flies. Circadian rhythms, commonly called *biorhythms,* are natural patterns of activity in an organism. These cycles have a period of about 24 hours. One familiar circadian rhythm is our wake-and-sleep cycle.

Whether space flight disrupts the circadian rhythms of organisms is important for space scientists to know, since it is well established that alterations in biorhythms

Ham, an early space pioneer.

affect human performance. Changes in circadian rhythms can also affect an organism's ability to eat, sleep, reproduce, and generally function effectively.

The purpose of this project is to determine the circadian rhythm of an organism.

You will need the following materials, equipment, and specimens: an animal that is interesting to study and relatively active, for example, a mouse, rat, gerbil, guinea pig, or even a fish (watching a bean plant for 24 hours isn't our idea of a good time!); cage or tank for the animal or fish; video camera and recorder (optional).

Prepare an environment where the animal will be comfortable but where it can be observed at all times.

Place the cage or tank in an area where the subject will have few distractions. A back room, storeroom, or basement is a good area as long as some sunlight can enter the room and there is good lighting.

You will now want to observe the organism *continual-ly* for a 24-hour period. Make observations on the activity level of the organism. This can be accomplished in one of two ways.

You and an assistant can share the task of observing the subject. Each of you can study the organism for time blocks of 2 to 4 hours. During the observation, you classify the nature of the activity that the organism is engaged in at regular time intervals. Below is a partial example of such a set of observations.

Time (Hours)	Description of Activity
0.0	Eating
0.1	Moving about cage, investigating
0.2	Moving about cage, rapidly
. . .	. . . .
23.8	Sleeping
23.9	Sleeping, starting to stir
24.0	Awake, moving toward food holder

You also can use a video camera to make your observations. This method has the advantage of not requiring constant attention and also allows for more complete and objective observations.

Obtain a video camera that records cassette tapes in the super-long-play (SLP) mode. Use standard 120 video cassettes. In this mode the tapes can record up to 6 hours of activity.

Once the taping of the 24-hour period is completed, the tapes can be reviewed and observations taken. This method has the added benefit of being able to move "fast-forward" through sleep periods and other inactive times.

From such observations, charts can be constructed to show the circadian cycles of the subject. Study the pattern of the organism that you have studied and determine its biorhythm. What are the periods of highest activity? Least activity? Can you predict when the subject will eat, sleep, defecate, and so on? Repeat the observation to confirm your predictions.

If you were planning to do an experiment with this subject and you wanted the animal to be most alert, during what time period would you schedule the experiment? If you wanted to handle the subject when it was the quietest, when would that be?

Find out if the following hypothesis is true or false: Scheduling activities of animals, including humans, in synchronization with their circadian rhythms can lead to better performance and less stress on the organism. You could change the subject to a 12- or 18-hour cycle and then test performance and behavior.

Observations can now be repeated under various sets of conditions. For example, artificial stimuli, changes in lighting direction and rotation, or vibration of the environment could be tested to see if they affect the circadian rhythm of the organism. What if the cage or tank were placed on a rotating turntable? Would this disrupt the normal circadian rhythm of the organism?

WHICH WAY IS UP?

Living organisms are complex, interactive systems of chemical, physical, physiological, and in the higher organisms, psychological processes. Plants and animals that have evolved in a one-G environment have adapted specialized mechanisms to detect the force of gravity. In the higher animals, these mechanisms usually involve specialized cells. Animals need to know "which way is up" at all times so that they can move about on the surface of the earth. What if the gravity is absent? Can animals function if there is no up or down?

The first student experiment flown on the space shuttle involved observing insect flight in a zero-gravity environment. The experiment, proposed by Todd E. Nelson, was simple in intent and design. The experimental procedure was to film three species of flying insects contained in an insect flight box on board the third space shuttle flight (STS-3).

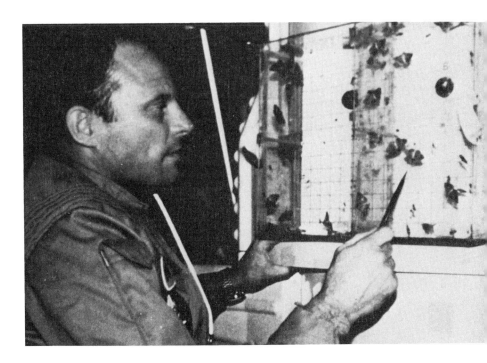

*Astronaut Jack R. Lousma holds insect flight
experiment aboard shuttle flight STS-3. The box
contained moths, bees, and flies. The flight
patterns of the insects were observed in zero-G.*

The basic question asked in this experiment was: How
do insects and other organisms know which way is up? In
other words, in the absence of a force pulling them
toward the center of mass of the earth, how do organisms orient themselves? Let's try to answer this question
by looking at two organisms that live in media different
from that in which we live—a fish and a plant.

DON'T FORGET YOUR LAB GOGGLES!

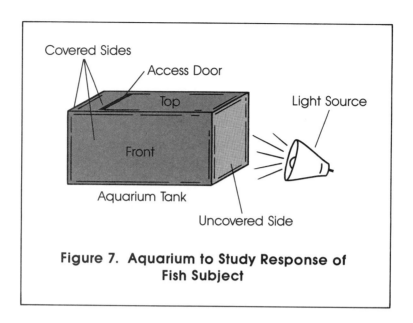

Figure 7. Aquarium to Study Response of Fish Subject

THE COCKEYED FISH

You will need the following materials, equipment, and specimens: a fish, two 3- to 5-gallon aquariums with covers, two bright light sources, black cloth or paper, scissors, clear plastic bag or container, and a camera.

With most species of fish, you will notice that the top, or dorsal, part of the fish is always colored darker than the bottom, or ventral, part. This is called countershading. The fish should have distinct countershading and be large enough to observe easily, at least ¾ inch (2 cm) long. A small fish from a nearby lake or stream is better than an aquarium-raised fish. Fish from the natural environment will have more distinct orientation tendencies and be less adapted to artificial stimuli.

You will be preparing the aquariums in different ways. One will be a kind of preliminary observation tank, the other the experimental tank.

Fill one aquarium with water and attach one light so that it illuminates the top. Put the fish into the tank.

Cover the other aquarium with black cloth or construction paper on the top and bottom and all sides except one. Leave one of the smaller sides of the aquarium uncovered.

Fill the aquarium with water. Place the light source so that it illuminates the uncovered side of the aquarium (see Figure 7). Also, figure a way to put the fish into the aquarium when the time comes.

While the fish is in the first aquarium, observe its movements and behavior. For example, does it rest near the bottom, top, or middle of the aquarium? How active is it? Does it bump up against the sides? Record all observations so that they can be used for comparison later.

Now transfer the fish to the covered tank. Make sure the light is coming directly from the side. Observe the fish carefully. Draw a sketch of the orientation at which the fish swims. Is the fish swimming as you expected it to? Continue to observe the fish and see if its behavior adapts to these mixed signals. If no gravity were present, how do you think the fish would behave? If there were no light? What if there were no light *or* gravity?

Place the small fish in the plastic container and fill the container completely with water. There should be no air bubbles in the container when you put on the top.

Turn the container slowly in different directions, even upside down. How does the fish orient itself with respect to gravity? By adjusting the buoyancy of their bodies, fish can create an upward force that balances out the pull of gravity. They can become "weightless." Does the fish sense the force of gravity even when it is "weightless"? How does the fish orient itself if the container is dropped in a free fall about 10 feet (3 m) or so?

Countershading is a camouflage mechanism that fish have evolved to make them harder to see in the water. Try photographing fish with the light coming from different directions to see how this affects the visibility of the fish in water. How are fish colored to counterbalance intense light coming from the surface of the water?

WHICH WAY IS DOWN?

Plants also exhibit tendencies to orient themselves with respect to light (phototropism) and gravity (geotropism). The mechanism for geotropism in plants is complex and not fully understood. Plant scientists hope that the study of plant behavior in zero-G will allow them to fully understand and control the geotropic response in plants. If it is found that certain species of plants cannot function in the zero-G environment of space, then some decisions must be made. Either replacements must be found for the food and/or materials that these organisms provide or an artificial gravity environment must be designed.

In this project, you will grow some plants and observe their response to changing gravitational direction.

You will need the following materials, equipment, and specimens: potting soil, square or rectangular box (wooden or plastic) at least 2 feet by 2 feet (70 cm × 70 cm), wire screen (enough to cover the top of the box), tape or tacks, small garden shovel, sharp knife or razor blade, low-power microscope. You also will need about a half-dozen plant seedlings. Corn seedlings, bean plants, pea plants, or oat seedlings should work well. The seedlings should be healthy and have roots at least 1 inch (2–3 cm) long. If you want to grow your own seedlings, consult a biology or gardening book. You could also obtain seedlings from a local greenhouse or a garden.

Place a layer of potting soil about 6 to 8 inches (15–20 cm) deep in the box. Plant the seedlings in the soil, distributing them evenly about the box. Now pack the soil down so that the surface is not loose. Spread the screen over the surface of the soil. Make holes in the screen just large enough for the seedlings to poke through. Secure the screen to the sides of the box with tape or tacks. Allow the plants to grow normally in good light for about 5 days. Water regularly but do not overwater—just enough to keep the soil moist.

After 5 days, stand the box on one of its sides (see Figure 8). Do this carefully to avoid losing soil or disturbing

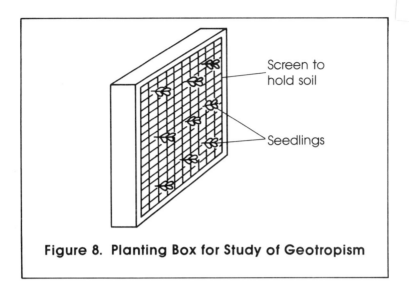

Figure 8. Planting Box for Study of Geotropism

the plants. Record the day on which you do this, and also record on which side the box is now resting. A good way to keep track is to number the sides (for example, 1, 2, 3, 4). Allow the plants to grow undisturbed for 5 more days. Keep light and moisture as normal as possible.

Repeat this process three more times until the box has been rotated to all four sides. Be sure to keep good records and record any observations that you may make about the growth of the plants out of the soil. If the plants seem healthy and you think the screen can hold the soil in place, you may even want to try growing the plants upside down for 5 days.

Following the growth period, use the shovel to remove the plants from the soil. Do this carefully so that you do not disturb the pattern of the roots. Gently wash the soil from the roots and place the plants on some absorbent paper. You may want to photograph the plants now for later study.

What is the appearance of the roots? Compare the growth of the roots with the periodic changes made in their orientation. Did the roots detect the changes in gravitational direction? What was their response? Is this response predictable? In other words, do the plants respond in a like manner during each change in orientation? How do you think the roots would respond if no gravity were present?

Take one of the roots with the most pronounced curvature and use the knife or razor blade to cut the root in half along its length. Place the root under a microscope and observe the plant cells in the roots. Look at the cells at a point where the root is bent or curved. Are the cells on the outside of the curve the same size (length) as the cells on the inside? What causes the root to curve? A certain plant hormone, abscisic acid (ABA), is known to inhibit plant cell growth and cause cells to be shorter. Find out whether the higher concentration of ABA would be on the inside or outside of a curved root. What do you think a zero-G environment would do to the distribution of ABA?

An interesting project can be done using plant hormones to artificially control the growth of roots. You could also study the effects of the removal of the root caps or of varying the direction from which light strikes the plant.

FLUIDS WORKING AGAINST GRAVITY

Many of the structures of living systems have evolved specifically to function within the gravity environment of earth. Some of these structures are needed to even survive the gravitational pull. Our skeletal system, for example, functions to hold our muscles and organs upright against their weight. Plants, too, have developed systems to work against gravity. How does a tall tree, for example, transport fluids to the uppermost reaches of its structure?

In this project, you will determine the speed at which plants can move fluids through their stems. Then you will determine if a change in gravity will alter the rate and pattern of the flow.

You will need the following materials and equipment: shallow pan, water, red food coloring, several stalks of fresh celery of about the same cross-sectional area, clock or watch, small knife, pencil, graph paper, plastic bottle or jar, wax candle, marking pen.

Fill the pan with about 1 inch (2–3 cm) of water. Add enough food coloring so that the water takes on a dark color. Use the knife to cut six equal lengths of celery about 5 inches (13 cm) long. Be sure the pieces of celery are all about the same in cross-section.

Stand the pieces of celery on their ends in the pan of colored water. Note the time. After 30 minutes, remove one of the celery stalks and determine the distance the colored fluid has moved up the stem. You may have to cut the stalk across its cross-section in order to determine the exact location of the fluid. Record the distance traveled in 30 minutes. Repeat this process every 30 minutes with another piece of celery until you have done all six. This should take 3 hours.

Graph the data you have collected. On the vertical axis, plot the distance traveled by the fluid through the stem. Plot the time on the horizontal axis. Draw a line connecting the points. If the points do not line up, draw in the straight line or curve that best fits the points.

You now will determine whether the celery stalk will transport liquids differently if it does not have to pull directly against gravity.

Cut another piece of celery identical to the others. Place the end of the stalk against the side of the plastic container about halfway up. Using the marking pen, outline the cross-section of the stalk on the side of the container. Remove the stalk. Then cut an opening in the plastic container slightly smaller than the outline you have just made. Cut carefully so as to produce smooth edges.

Wedge the stalk into the opening so it protrudes into the container about 1 inch (25 mm). The stalk should fit snugly into the opening. Seal any gaps around the stalk by dripping candle wax around the opening. Pour some of the colored liquid into the container. The level of the liquid should not be more than ½ inch (13 mm) above the protruding stalk. Note the time. Let the container stand for 50 minutes. Periodically during this time, observe the movement of the liquid through the celery.

According to your graph, how far would you expect the liquid to travel through the stalk in 50 minutes if it was upright?

After 50 minutes, measure the distance that the liquid has traveled. If you can see this through the stalk, mark the distance with a pen. You can measure it later. Let it stand another 50 minutes.

After 100 minutes total time, remove the stalk from the container and measure the total distance covered. How does it compare with the distance predicted by the graph? Is this what you expected? Now cut the celery stalk at the farthest point that the liquid traveled. Is the flow front of the liquid straight across, that is, perpendicular to its length? Can you explain this observation?

Do you think celery would grow in space? Would it grow better or worse than on earth?

Find out if air pressure affects the speed at which the liquid flows. Try other plant stalks such as those of flowers or other garden vegetables. Try other liquids such as sugar solutions of different concentrations or alcohol or glycerol.

CREATING MARS ON EARTH

One of the most intriguing questions concerning space exploration is whether there is life on other planets. The Viking spacecraft sent to Mars were designed to land on the Martian surface and to test for the possibility of life on "the red planet." Lunar soil was tested for the presence of microorganisms and organic chemicals, the building blocks of life. Intelligent life may well be present in other solar systems, but if there is any life in our solar system,

Top: Photograph of the Martian surface taken by the Viking 1 lander in 1976 (you can see part of the craft in the middle of the picture). The large boulder at the left is about 3 feet by 10 feet (1 m by 3 m). Bottom: A view of the Martian surface from Viking 2 (1976). Two scans by one of the cameras were combined to produce the picture. The rock in the lower right-hand corner is 10 inches (25 cm) across. The largest rock near the center of the picture is about 2 feet (61 cm) long and 1 foot (30 cm) high.

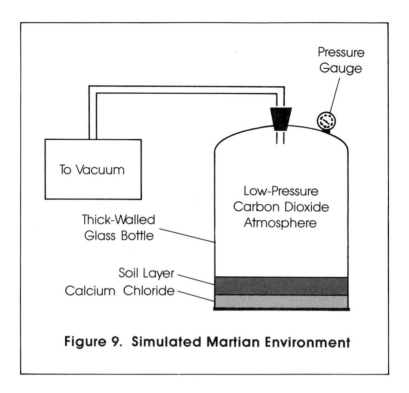

Figure 9. Simulated Martian Environment

other than on earth, it will probably be limited to microorganisms.

What exactly would an organism have to endure to exist on Mars, the most hospitable planet (other than Earth) in our solar system? Could any Earth organisms survive there?

The intent of this project is to simulate the conditions on Mars. We will then place some Earth organisms in this environment and see if they survive; and if they do survive, for how long.

The equipment suggested for this project can become quite involved and may be beyond what you are capable of obtaining. However, if you can simulate just some of the conditions described, you will be able to better understand the obstacles to the establishment on other planets of life as we know it.

You will need the following materials and equipment: sandy soil, large, thick-walled glass bottle that can be sealed, sunlamp, vacuum pump with hoses and valves, 18 ounces (500 g) of calcium chloride ($CaCl_2$), source of dry carbon dioxide (CO_2) (gas cylinder), small bottle.

Mars has a dry, carbon dioxide atmosphere. The atmospheric pressure is low (10 percent of Earth's at the surface) and may vary in temperature from −90°F to 80°F (−70°C to 30°C). Martian soil is similar in chemical composition to Earth's. It is sandy and dry. Mars is also extremely windy.

How closely you simulate these conditions will depend on your imagination and the equipment available. Figure 9 illustrates a possible setup. The soil should be baked in an oven at 230°F (110°C) for several hours prior to use. The calcium chloride layer will maintain a low humidity in the bottle. You can simulate temperature extremes using a sunlamp and a refrigerator freezer. Study pictures from the Viking landings and data from Martian exploration to obtain more detail.

Once you have created a suitable Martian environment, choose an organism to test. Microorganisms such as molds, algae, and fungi would be most realistic. Simple plants and seeds, as well as insects, could be used. **DO NOT TEST MAMMALS OR OTHER VERTEBRATES, AND MAKE SURE ANY INSECTS YOU USE ARE NOT RARE OR ENDANGERED SPECIES (SOME BUTTERFLIES ARE).** Two samples of the organism should be available so that one can be grown in a normal environment and used for comparison.

Test the organisms under different conditions, first one at a time, then in different combinations, and finally all together. First, find out the effect of the sunlamp, which is rich in ultraviolet light. How are the organisms affected? Are their growth rates altered? Is there any reproduction? What are the offspring like?

Next, study the effects of temperature extremes. Martian days are about the same as those on Earth, but the nights would be very cold. Find out how such temperature extremes would influence your organisms.

*A closeup view of Arabella, one of the
two spiders aboard Skylab 3, and the web
it had spun in zero-gravity environment. The
experiment that Arabella was part of was
proposed by 17-year-old Judith S. Miles,
of Lexington, Massachusetts.*

Since there is little atmosphere on Mars, there is little
protection from radiation. You could take your organisms
to a lab and have them bombarded with radiation and
then tested in the Martian environment. A local college,
university, or special laboratory probably can help you
with this. You might even try your dentist, who probably
has an X-ray machine in the office.

You can simulate the Martian atmosphere by evacu-
ating the large bottle, then allowing a small amount of
carbon dioxide gas to enter the bottle so that the pressure inside is no more than 70 to 80 mm/Hg (1.8 PSI).

What are the chances of an organism adapted to the Earth environment surviving in the harsh simulated Martian environment? If humans eventually colonize Mars, what provisions will be required to protect them from the Martian environment? In the small glass bottle, construct an environment that could sustain your organisms in the simulated Martian environment. Another interesting project would be to design a model Martian settlement. Either draw such a structure or construct a model out of clay or wood. You may be designing a city of the future!

HOME SWEET HOME

The earth is about 4.6 billion years old. Life as we know it has been present for about 600 million years. This life has evolved and adapted to the special environment of the earth. Humans have adapted to the various conditions on the surface of our planet. As we look to our new frontier, space, we may well consider what provisions must be made in order for life to survive and even thrive. Perhaps as plants, animals, and humans establish themselves in space, new adaptations will occur. What types of organisms do *you* think evolution will favor in the environment of space?

7

HUMAN BEINGS
IN SPACE

Many of the first questions about human space flight have been answered. Humans can survive the launch, prolonged zero-G conditions, and the reentry in a properly designed vehicle. Astronauts can eat, sleep, work, and think clearly in the space environment, provided they are trained for the conditions they will encounter.

Space scientists were, and still are, concerned with the possible negative effects of space flight. Considerations include takeoff acceleration, disorientation caused by vibration during launch and reentry, isolation and confinement, changes in daily body cycles, prolonged weightlessness, motion sickness, radiation, and changing nutritional needs. Scientists also are concerned about the possibility of exposure to extraterrestrial organisms—organisms that originate away from the earth.

As spacecraft design improves and we become more knowledgeable about the effects of space flight on humans, space flight will be possible for more and more people. Space flight will become increasingly commonplace, no longer restricted to a highly trained core of elite astronauts. Each person, in turn, must learn of the rigors of space flight. In this chapter, we will simulate some of the conditions found during a space flight and look at some of the problems associated with these conditions.

EXPERIENCING CHANGES
IN GRAVITY

Our sense of falling, rising, and acceleration is centered in small organs located in our inner ear. These organs are composed of small, nerve-lined chambers containing small mineral crystals called *otoliths.* As our bodies are accelerated, the otoliths press against the nerves on the side of the chambers and we sense motion.

Our sense of spatial orientation is also controlled by organs in our inner ear called semicircular canals. These are fluid-filled canals arranged in three planes: lateral, horizontal, and vertical. Changes in the position of our head cause the fluid in these canals to flow differently. We can detect changes in rotational acceleration, which amounts to changes in spin rate.

In this project, we will look at ways of experiencing weightlessness as well as increased G-forces and determine if such experiences affect coordination or orientation. You will not need any special equipment for this project, but you may need to go to a park, playground, swimming pool, or amusement park in order to experience the effects.

In order to make this project suitable for a science fair, you will need to keep careful records of all data collected and possibly take photographs of the tests performed. Make sure you state what you are trying to prove or disprove with the activities that you perform. For example, "Riding on a merry-go-round will not affect how you walk" is an example of a testable hypothesis.

Before we experience changes in acceleration, we need to have some simple tests of coordination and orientation. Try these three tests:

1. Walk a straight line for 20 feet (5–6 m). Both feet should stay on the line. Try it with your eyes open and then closed.

2. Extend your arms out to each side. Touch your nose with your index finger. Alternate with your left and right finger twenty times. Try this with your eyes open, then closed.

3. Stand on one foot. Bend over and touch your toes. Try this with the other foot. Try this with your eyes open and then closed.

You should have little difficulty performing these feats. We will use them to test your coordination during and following changes in acceleration.

A good way to experience weightlessness for a short time is in free fall. You can experience free fall by jumping from a diving board into a swimming pool filled with water. While you are falling, there is little net gravitational force on you. As you are falling, test your orientation using the nose-touching test.

You can experience increased simulated G-forces by riding on a small merry-go-round at a local playground. The outward force caused by the spinning will act on your body. The spinning will also cause disorientation. After riding on the merry-go-round for 20 to 30 seconds, try the three orientation tests.

Perhaps the best place to simulate the effects of launch, reentry, and weightlessness is at a large amusement park. Several of the rides subject you to negative and positive accelerations. A roller coaster, for example, subjects passengers to several seconds of near free fall. Study each of the rides to determine what forces the ride will subject you to. Choose three or four different rides. During the ride, be aware of the forces applied to you.

At what points in the ride are you under increased acceleration? When do you experience weightlessness? During the ride, try the nose-touching test, but make sure you observe all safety rules and do not extend your arms outside the ride.

Immediately after the ride, perform the three tests of coordination. Have a friend observe you. Did the stimulation of the ride affect your orientation or coordination? Try this with several types of rides. Do certain types of stimuli disturb your orientation more than others? Are the

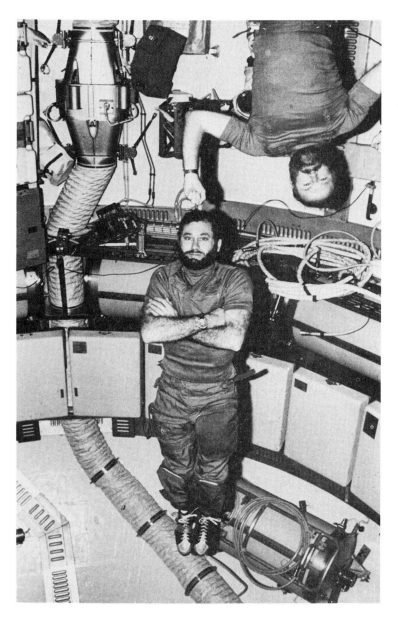

Astronauts William Pouge (in middle) and Gerald Carr aboard Skylab demonstrating effects of zero-G.

effects the same for everyone? Are some people more or less prone to the disorienting effects of such stimuli?

You might try to see if you can be "trained" to walk a straight line after a violent merry-go-round ride. Try to see if different individuals react in different ways to the amount of training.

When astronauts are being selected and tested, they are subjected to many tests to determine their suitability for space flight. They experience weightlessness for short periods through the use of a special aircraft. The plane is put into a parabolic free-fall flight path similar to that of an orbiting spacecraft. During this time, the astronauts can experience as much as 30 seconds of weightlessness similar to the free fall on a roller coaster. They also can experience increased G-forces using centrifugal force and linear acceleration devices. In this way, astronauts can simulate the stimuli they will experience during a space flight and learn to function effectively.

A WHOLE LOTTA SHAKIN'

In addition to the acceleration and deceleration astronauts experience during launches and reentry, they are also subjected to large amounts of vibrations. Studies have shown that human reaction time is affected by prolonged vibrational stimuli. How much it is affected depends upon the individual and the type and amount of vibration. A simple experiment can determine a person's reaction to vibrational stress.

You will need the following materials and equipment: large chair (preferably unpadded with arms and a straight back); four pieces of rubber or sponge material to place under the legs of the chair, dense enough so that someone sitting in the chair will not be in solid contact with the floor; large towel or wide belt; meter stick; blindfold; camera. You will also need the help of two or three other people.

Keep careful records of all data that you collect, and photograph the equipment you use. Try to predict the effects of the vibrations on your performance.

Place the chair on the pieces of rubber material. Do this so that the chair is not in solid contact with the floor and can be vibrated by shaking its legs. The rubber material should be dense enough to allow someone to sit in the chair and still not be in solid contact with the floor. Have the "subject" sit in the chair and secure him or her using the belt or towel. The subject should be comfortable but firmly held into the chair.

We now want to test the subject's normal reaction time. Have the subject place his or her forearm on the arm of the chair. The subject's hand should extend beyond the arm of the chair. Hold the meter stick vertically in front of the subject so that the bottom of the stick is at the level of the subject's hand. The meter stick should be held such that it will pass the index finger and the thumb of the subject. Instruct the subject to catch the meter stick as soon as he or she sees it begin to fall.

Record how far the meter stick falls before it is caught. This is a measure of reaction time to visual stimuli. Repeat the test several times in order to determine an average reaction time.

Now repeat the test with the subject blindfolded. This time when the stick is dropped provide some sort of audible signal such as a voice command or mechanical noise maker. Again, repeat the test several times to determine an average reaction time to sound stimuli.

We now want to compare these results with the reaction time of the subject under vibrational stimuli. Have one or two helpers gently but uniformly shake the chair. The shaking should be continued for several minutes. While the subject is still being vibrated, repeat the tests as you did before.

What effect did the vibration have on reaction time? Try changing some of the variables such as length and magnitude of the vibrations, uniformity of the shaking, and which hand is used. Try other types of stimuli. Will loud noise or bright lights affect the reaction time? What is the combined effect? Are all subjects affected in the same way?

Reaction time is a critical characteristic for an astronaut. Astronauts must be able to respond to situations that may be encountered during a space flight. Subjecting astronauts to stress-causing stimuli is another way to prepare them for space flight.

Can an individual be "trained" to withstand the effects of vibration?

FOOD FOR SPACE

Prolonged space flight, of course, requires that the astronauts eat and drink in space. How is this accomplished in the zero-G environment? Obviously one cannot fill a glass of milk or put a spoonful of peas on a plate.

Food for space must be prepared in such a way as to accomplish three objectives. First, it must be able to be conveniently and efficiently stored, eaten, and disposed of in zero-G. Second, it must fulfill the minimum nutritional requirements of the crew members. Third, it must be appetizing and appealing to the astronauts. This last criterion has been shown to be very important to maintaining crew morale and thus positive working conditions on long space flights.

The following projects will deal with some of these problems and challenges.

CALORIE INPUT AND OUTPUT

In this project, you will keep a record of your daily intake of *Calories* from the foods you eat. A Calorie (capital "C") is a measure of the energy content of foods that you eat. You will estimate the number of Calories that you expend during a normal day's activities. You can then measure your Calorie intake versus output and compare them with those of an astronaut functioning in space.

You will need the following materials and equipment: list of common foods and their Calorie content (many cookbooks contain such information), small notebook, pencil, watch.

Start recording your nutritional data at a time when you will be following a more or less regular schedule, for

Food packages for Gemini 7 space flight back in 1965. This was the complete food supply for the two-man crew for a fourteen-day mission. Could you assemble a food pack of similar dimensions?

example, going to school each day, eating at about the same time, sleeping normally. Record each food item that you eat each day. Estimate how much you eat. Using the Calorie counter or the information on the nutritional labels found on most packages, determine the Calorie content of each food item. At the end of each day, determine the total intake.

Continue recording Calorie intake for at least a week. After this period, determine the average daily Calorie intake by dividing the total Calories consumed by the number of days that you kept records.

Find out how many Calories per day the average astronaut will require on a normal space flight. This amount will vary a great deal depending on the individual, the activities involved, and conditions aboard the spacecraft. The Calorie requirements of an individual in the one-G environment of earth may vary also. Some activities (for example, strenuous exercise) require more energy than others.

You can estimate your Calorie requirements by looking up the information in tables that give the intake requirements depending on your weight as well as the activity in which you are engaged. How does your daily Calorie intake compare to your estimated requirements? Remember, these numbers are only estimates and should not be used as a way of controlling diet.

It is critical for space scientists to closely match the nutritional intake of the astronauts with their actual requirements in space. The nutritional needs of the crew must be fully met in order for them to function efficiently in space.

It is also important not to overestimate the requirements of the crew. Not only may this result in undesirable weight gains but in the transportation of unneeded amounts of supplies. It has been determined that an overestimation of the Calorie needs of only 300 Calories per day for a four-person crew for one year would require 338 pounds (150 kg) of unnecessary food supplies to be included in the spacecraft. This would require more fuel, storage space, and disposal space. All are in critically short supply in a spacecraft.

Calorie intake is just one of the nutritional requirements that can be studied. Similar studies can be done on carbohydrate, fat, protein, and vitamin intake. You may want to estimate your consumption of other various nutritional components by using the nutritional information found on the packaging of foods.

Other areas can be investigated. How much water per day is required for an astronaut? Measure your total water input and output. An analysis of water loss from the body could be made, by placing a watertight bag over the arm and hand and measuring the perspiration from the skin. Air could be allowed to flow through the bag and the water captured in a drying agent.

Temperature rise might also be considered as it relates to conditions produced inside space suits. How much oxygen is used each day by an astronaut, and how much carbon dioxide is given off? You could design equipment to make these measurements. What is the source of oxygen, and what happens to all the carbon dioxide on an extended space flight?

THE WHOLE PACKAGE

Packaging, preparing, and consuming food in the weightless environment is a challenging problem for space scientists.

Imagine yourself "sitting down" in a zero-G environment for supper as you normally have it, at a table with plates, silverware, and glasses. Everything is floating! Your milk is wetting the inside of the glass and floating in a large drop. You can't quite get hold of the meat, and when you try to cut it with a knife and fork you get no leverage. The peas are simple enough; just pick them out of the air one at a time and pop them in your mouth. We won't mention what happens to the mashed potatoes and gravy! And before you worry about who's going to do the dishes, you have to catch them first.

The first space flights, in Project Mercury, were short enough that food was not a problem. When Project Gemini flights were proposed with durations of up to 14 days, new techniques had to be developed to prepare meals for the crews. Many of the convenience foods that you can buy in grocery stores were developed for space flight. One example is one-portion cans of pudding, which were developed for easy consumption. The pull-ring top is easy to open. The pudding is thick and sticky enough to stay in the can and to adhere to a spoon until eaten. Many other examples of such "food packaging engineering" can be found in stores.

EATING A MEAL IN SPACE

In this project, you will plan and eat a space meal. In so doing, you will have to consider many of the unique problems of eating in the weightless environment.

Your materials will vary a great deal, but some things that you will need are: a large tray, plastic bags, rubber bands, pieces of Velcro fastener, glue, milk, various food items, and a large sponge (to help clean up the mess).

First, plan what you want to eat. Don't worry too much about the nutritional content of the meal. We are more concerned with the mechanics of eating it. The meal should be complete and contain about 1,000 Calories.

Then design a way to drink liquids in zero-G. A good test of the drinking device is to try to drink while hanging upside down without spilling any of the liquid. A look at some of the commercially available fruit and soft drinks might give you some ideas. The device must be self-contained, sanitary, and easy to use.

Next, design a food tray that can be used to hold your space meal. When you are not handling a utensil or piece of food, the tray must be secured somewhere so it doesn't float freely about the cabin.

Now let's put together our meal. Many commercially available foods are appropriate for space flights. As you choose foods for your meal, here are some basic guidelines and hints:

1. Water, hot and cold, is available. However, the water must be able to be injected, not poured, into the food container.

2. A knife cannot be used because the cut pieces would drift around the cabin. Food must be in bite-sized pieces.

3. Foods that will stick to a spoon can be eaten.

4. Foods that can be stuck on a fork are also practical if they can be contained.

5. Provisions must be made for convenient disposal of waste. Ideally the containers should have some practical use.

A little ingenuity will allow you to put together a meal similar to that eaten by astronauts in space. As you eat the meal, try to keep in mind the weightless conditions in space.

Now design a complete menu for a period of 1 day, 1 month, and 1 year for one person. If you are interested in backpacking and are planning a camping trip, this menu can be fun and rewarding and you could test your menu on the trip. Remember to keep the weight and volume of the food as low as possible.

Eating in space is but one of the practical problems the space scientist must consider. Sleeping, brushing your teeth, shaving, urinating, defecating, bathing, and just plain relaxing are all processes or procedures that must be carefully considered when planning for extended space flight. Human engineering must be considered when designing the working environment of the spacecraft.

We have advanced well beyond the initial goal of surviving in space. The people of the earth are now set to accomplish the task of living, working, and inhabiting space for longer and longer times.

8

PREPARING FOR
THE UNIMAGINED

How can you prepare to do something that nobody has ever done before? How did Columbus prepare to sail to the New World? How did Roald Amundsen prepare for the first journey to the South Pole? What about the pioneers in space flight such as Allan Shepard and Neil Armstrong? How did they prepare themselves for their first-time accomplishments? Can the space explorers of tomorrow prepare to accomplish feats that now cannot even be imagined? This is the challenge facing the space scientist.

Tomorrow's explorers must attempt to learn what is presently known about our world and outer space. In addition, they must be aware of the theories that predict the nature of things not yet known. However, they must not be bound by these. Space scientists use science as a tool to adapt present knowledge as new discoveries are made. This is the true strength of the scientific method. It provides a framework and plan to test, understand, and predict the nature of new phenomena.

In the beginning of this book, we discussed the method of science. You were encouraged to use this method in each of the projects and explorations that were presented to you. You should now look to the future to projects not yet imagined, and become tomorrow's explorers.

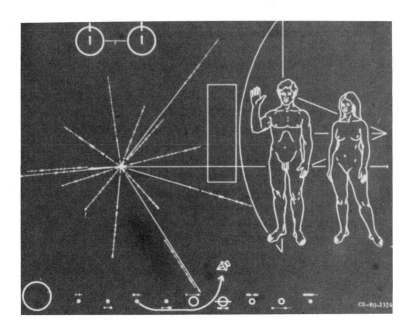

The plaque aboard the Pioneer 10 spacecraft. The plaque was designed by Frank Drake and Carl Sagan. Pioneer 10, which was launched in March 1972, is the first human-made object to leave the solar system. The symbols and pictures on the plaque were designed to convey information about our civilization, solar system, and galaxy to any beings from other worlds who might encounter the spacecraft. The picture of the man and woman shows what we look like; the man's hand is raised in a gesture of greeting. Our sun and the planets of our solar system are lined up at the bottom. The spacecraft is shown leaving the third planet, earth. The figure in the upper left represents a hydrogen atom; the distance between the two atoms is a universal unit of measurement. The starlike figure depicts our galaxy, with lines drawn to represent pulsars—stars whose energy emissions fluctuate.

What might be just beyond what we know? Earth is presently monitoring the far reaches of space for signals from other life-forms. What would these life-forms be like, if they exist? How do we communicate with them or even contact them.

What will they be able to teach us? Will they be a threat to us or will they benefit our society? Now such questions are only theoretical, but someday they may need to be answered.

If we are indeed going to attempt interstellar travel, whole new technologies are going to need to be developed. Traveling such distances with today's most advanced chemical rockets is impossible! Matter-antimatter drive systems, presently existing only in the realm of science fiction or theory, will perhaps be the mode of transport in the future.

The Pioneer spacecraft were our first attempt to travel beyond our solar system. Humankind has used a robot as its ambassador to other worlds because of the limitations of the frail and short-lived human body. If humans are ever to travel the vast time and distance of space, these limitations must be overcome. A spacecraft must be designed to allow a human to withstand far greater accelerations than they are now capable of. In addition, a form of suspended animation may be needed to extend the time frame available to human space travelers.

Great advances in knowledge and understanding have often been as a result of technological developments. We won't know what we will find or even what to look for until we have the tools to do the looking. It is the challenge of tomorrow's space scientists to develop those tools and look just beyond what can now be imagined.

GLOSSARY

Alloy. A mixture of two metals melted together.

Biorhythm. See Circadian Rhythm.

Buoyant Force. A force on an immersed object in a fluid caused by differences in densities between the object and the fluid.

Calorie. A unit of heat equivalent to 1,000 small calories, which is the quantity of heat required to raise the temperature of 1 gram of water 1 degree Celsius.

Centripetal Force. The force necessary to keep an object moving in a circular path.

Circadian Rhythm. Occurring in twenty-four-hour cycles.

Composite. Made up of distinct parts.

Compound. A pure substance made up of two or more elements combined chemically.

Convection. A circulation of a fluid caused by density differences and gravity.

Density. The ratio of the mass of a substance divided by its volume.

Dependent Variable. A variable whose value is determined by that of one or more other variables.

Diffusion. The process of molecules of gases spreading out spontaneously.

Electromagnetic Radiation. All forms of radiant energy that move as waves.

Electrophoresis. The movement of suspended particles through a fluid under the action of an electric field.

Floating Zone. A molten region in a cylindrical rod formed by heating the rod at a given point.

Floc. A mass formed by the aggregation of a number of fine suspended particles.

Floccing. The process of forming a floc.

Fractional Distillation. The process of separating liquids by a difference of their boiling points.

Free Fall. The condition of unrestrained motion in a gravitational field.

Geomagnetic Field. The magnetic field that surrounds the earth.

Gravitational Mass. The mass of a material as determined on a conventional laboratory balance.

Hydrostatic Pressure. The force per unit area exerted by a liquid on an immersed object.

Hypothesis. A plausible explanation based on inference from observed data.

Independent Variable. The phenomenon that is manipulated by the experimenter during an experiment.

Inertia. A property of matter by which it tends to remain at rest or tends to remain in uniform motion unless acted on by an outside force.

Inertial Balance. A device used to measure the amount of mass in an object.

Inertial Mass. The mass of an object as determined by an inertial balance.

Ion Migration. The movement of ions in an electric field.

Magnetosphere. A region of the upper atmosphere that surrounds the earth and is dominated by the earth's magnetic field.

Mass. The quantity of matter in an object.

Materials Science. The application of scientific principles to the investigation of relationships between the structure and properties of materials.

One-G. A condition where the acceleration due to gravity or other force is the same as the earth's gravity.

Otolith. A calcareous concretion in the internal ear of a vertebrate.

Secondary Cell. A cell that can store electrical energy in the form of chemical energy.

Sedimentation. The process of forming or depositing sediment.

Surface Tension. A condition caused by intermolecular forces which resembles that of an elastic skin on the surface of a liquid.

Suspension. The state of a substance when its particles are mixed with but undissolved in a fluid or solid.

Theory. An acceptable general principle offered to explain a phenomenon.

Variable. A quantity that may assume any one of a set of values.

Weightlessness. A condition in which no acceleration, whether caused by gravity or by any other force, can be detected.

APPENDIX
ONE

COMPUTER
PROGRAMS

The following computer programs were written to help you with the calculations for the inertial balance project in Chapter 2. The programs were written for the Apple II computer but should work on most systems using the BASIC language. HOME—which clears the screen and places the cursor at the top of the screen—is different on different machines. If you use any of these programs, test them with the data that appears in Appendix Two. Different computer systems may give different results and you may have some problems.

Program 1 is a calibration program that determines the apparent mass of the ruler and tape. The value that Program 1 calculates is in penny units. Record it in a notebook, since you'll need its value for Programs 2 and 3. If standard masses are available, you can calibrate the balance in grams or other units as long as the ratio of the calibration masses is 1 to 2.

```
100 REM   PROGRAM 1
110 HOME
120 PRINT "THIS PROGRAM WILL DETERMINE THE MASS"
130 PRINT "(M) OF THE RULER AND THE TAPE FOR THE"
140 PRINT "INERTIAL BALANCE EXPERIMENT."
150 PRINT
```

```
160 REM   ASK FOR THE AVERAGE TIME FOR THE 10
PENNIES AND THE 20 PENNIES
170 PRINT "TYPE IN THE AVERAGE TIME FOR"
180 PRINT "20 SWINGS IN SECONDS"
190 PRINT "WITH 10 PENNIES ON THE BALANCE."
200 INPUT T1
210 PRINT : PRINT
220 PRINT "TYPE IN THE AVERAGE TIME FOR"
230 PRINT "20 SWINGS IN SECONDS"
240 PRINT "WITH 20 PENNIES ON THE BALANCE."
250 INPUT T2
260 REM   CALCULATE THE VALUE OF M
270 M = (10 * ((T2 * T2) − 2 * (T1 * T1)))/((T1 * T1) −
(T2 * T2))
280 REM ROUND OFF THE VALUE TO 4 SIGNIFICANT
FIGURES
290 M = INT (M * 1000 + .5)/1000
300 PRINT: PRINT
310 PRINT "THE VALUE OF M IN PENNY UNITS IS "; M
320 END
```

Program 2 requires the apparent mass of the ruler and tape from Program 1. Program 2 determines the mass of some unknown objects (nickels) in penny units and then finds the ratio of the mass of one nickel to the mass of one penny. If the balance is calibrated in other units such as grams, the program can be modified to calculate the mass of unknown objects in grams.

```
100 REM   PROGRAM 2
110 HOME
120 PRINT "THIS PROGRAM WILL DETERMINE THE MASS
OF"
130 PRINT "10 NICKELS IN PENNY UNITS."
140 PRINT
150 PRINT "TYPE IN THE VALUE IN PENNY UNITS YOU"
160 PRINT "DETERMINED FOR THE MASS OF THE RULER"
170 PRINT "AND THE TAPE (M) FROM PROGRAM 1."
180 INPUT M
```

```
190 PRINT
200 PRINT "TYPE IN THE AVERAGE TIME FOR 20 SWINGS"
210 PRINT "IN SECONDS WITH 10 NICKELS TAPED TO"
220 PRINT "THE BALANCE."
230 INPUT T2
240 PRINT
250 PRINT "TYPE IN THE AVERAGE TIME FOR 20 SWINGS"
260 PRINT "IN SECONDS WITH 10 PENNIES TAPED TO"
270 PRINT "THE BALANCE."
280 INPUT T1
290 PRINT
300 REM   CALCULATE THE MASS OF 10 NICKELS IN
PENNY UNITS
310 N = (10 * T2 * T2 + M * T2 * T2 − M * T1 * T1)/(T1 *
T1)
320 REM   ROUND OFF THE VALUE TO 4 SIGNIFICANT
FIGURES
330 N = INT (N * 100 + .5)/100
340 PRINT
350 PRINT "THE MASS OF 10 NICKELS IN PENNY UNITS IS "
360 PRINT N
370 REM   CALCULATE THE RATIO OF THE MASS OF 1
NICKEL TO THE MASS OF 1 PENNY
380 PRINT
390 PRINT "THE MASS RATIO OF 1 NICKEL TO"
400 PRINT "1 PENNY ON THE INERTIAL BALANCE IS "
410 PRINT N/10
420 END
```

Program 3 requires the apparent mass of the ruler and tape from Program 1. Program 3 determines the mass of some unknown objects (dimes) in penny units and then calculates the ratio of the mass of one dime to the mass of one penny.

```
100 REM   PROGRAM 3
110 HOME
120 PRINT "THIS PROGRAM WILL DETERMINE THE MASS
OF"
```

```
130 PRINT "10 DIMES IN PENNY UNITS."
140 PRINT
150 PRINT "TYPE IN THE VALUE IN PENNY UNITS YOU"
160 PRINT "DETERMINED FOR THE MASS OF THE RULER"
170 PRINT "AND THE TAPE (M) FROM PROGRAM 1."
180 INPUT M
190 PRINT
200 PRINT "TYPE IN THE AVERAGE TIME FOR 20 SWINGS"
210 PRINT "IN SECONDS WITH 10 DIMES TAPED TO"
220 PRINT "THE BALANCE."
230 INPUT T2
240 PRINT
250 PRINT "TYPE IN THE AVERAGE TIME FOR 20 SWINGS"
260 PRINT "IN SECONDS WITH 10 PENNIES TAPED TO"
270 PRINT "THE BALANCE."
280 INPUT T1
290 PRINT
300 REM   CALCULATE THE MASS OF 10 DIMES IN PENNY
UNITS
310 D = (10 * T2 * T2 + M * T2 * T2 − M * T1 * T1)/(T1 *
T1)
320 REM ROUND OFF THE VALUE TO 4 SIGNIFICANT
FIGURES
330 D = INT (D * 100 + .5)/100
340 PRINT
350 PRINT "THE MASS OF 10 DIMES IN PENNY UNITS IS "
360 PRINT D
370 REM   CALCULATE THE RATIO OF THE MASS OF 1
DIME TO THE MASS OF 1 PENNY
380 PRINT
390 PRINT "THE MASS RATIO OF 1 DIME TO"
400 PRINT "1 PENNY ON THE INERTIAL BALANCE IS "
410 PRINT D/10
420 END
```

Program 4 was written for the Spaceships, Hot and Cold project in Chapter 3. This program will only work on the Apple II computer and requires that a thermistor be connected to the game I/O port inside the computer. The program draws a graph on the Hi Res Screen of the relationship between the temperature of a substance and time.

```
100 REM   PROGRAM 4
110 REM   THIS PROGRAM REQUIRES THAT A THERMISTOR
BE CONNECTED TO PINS 1 AND 6 ON THE GAME I/O
CONNECTOR INSIDE THE APPLE II COMPUTER
120 REM   TIME SETS DELAY TIME BETWEEN READINGS
130 TIME = 1000
140 REM   SET HIRES GRAPHICS AND COLOR
150 HGR
160 HCOLOR = 3
170 REM   DRAW BORDER AROUND GRAPHICS AREA
180 HPLOT 0,0 TO 259,0 TO 259,159 TO 1,159 TO 1,1
190 REM   SETS FULL SCREEN GRAPHICS
200 POKE 16302,0
210 REM   READS THERMISTOR RESISTANCE
220 REM   PLOTS RESISTANCE ON SCREEN
230 FOR X = 1 TO 259
240 Y = PDL (0)
250 HPLOT TO X,Y − 20
260 FOR I = 0 TO TIME
270 NEXT I
280 NEXT X
290 REM   DOES NOT START OVER UNTIL A RETURN IS
PRESSED
300 INPUT Y$
310 GOTO 150
320 END
```

APPENDIX
TWO

TEST DATA

The following data actually collected by the authors for the inertial balance project are intended to be test data to check Programs 1, 2, and 3 in Appendix One. The average times for the 10 pennies and then the 20 pennies should give an apparent mass of the ruler and the tape of 7.521 penny units.

Calibration Data Table

Time for 20 swings with 10 pennies
Trial #1	14.45 sec
Trial #2	14.45 sec
Trial #3	14.47 sec
Average	14.45 sec

Time for 20 swings with 20 pennies
Trial #1	18.13 sec
Trial #2	18.07 sec
Trial #3	18.13 sec
Average	18.11 sec

The following data for nickels and dimes can be used to check Programs 2 and 3 to see that they are working properly. Program 2 should calculate that a nickel is 1.722 times more massive than a penny with this test data. Program 3 should calculate that a dime is 0.791 times as massive as a penny with the test data.

Nickel/Dime Data Table

Time for 20 swings with 10 nickels

Trial #1	17.13 sec
Trial #2	17.18 sec
Trial #3	17.19 sec
Average	17.17 sec

Time for 20 swings with 10 dimes

Trial #1	13.59 sec
Trial #2	13.54 sec
Trial #3	13.54 sec
Average	13.56 sec

APPENDIX
THREE

SOURCES, REFERENCES, AND ORGANIZATIONS

SOURCES OF MATERIALS
FOR EXPERIMENTS

Edmund Scientific Company, 101 East Gloucester Pike, Barrington, N.J. 08007. (800) 257-6173

Fenwal Electronics, 63 Fountain Street, Framingham, Mass. 01701 (Source of themistors for temperature measurement)

Radio Shack/Tandy Corporation, 1800 One Tandy Center, Fort Worth, Tex. 76102 (Excellent sources for small electronic parts)

Your local pharmacist may be able to help you get chemicals that you need. Usually you will need direct adult supervision to obtain chemicals in this way.

Your local hobby store may be an excellent source for chemicals, glassware, and other supplies. The owner may be able to special-order materials for you.

If you can get your science teacher interested in a particular project, your school may be able to lend you the equipment you need. You may have to do the project in school under the direct supervision of the teacher if you use school equipment or supplies.

MAGAZINES

Astronomy, P. O. Box 92788, 625 East St. Paul Avenue, Milwaukee, Wisc. 53202

Aviation Week & Space Technology, McGraw-Hill, Inc., P.O. Box 430, Hightstown, N.J. 08520

Commercial Space, 1221 Avenue of the Americas, New York, N.Y. 10020

Computer & Electronics, Ziff Davis Publishing Company, 1 Park Avenue, New York, N.Y. 10016

Current Health, 1 and *2,* Curriculum Innovation, 3500 Western Avenue, Highland Park, Ill. 60035

Popular Electronics, Ziff-Davis Publishing Co., 1 Park Avenue, New York, N.Y. 10016

Popular Science, 380 Madison Avenue, New York, N.Y. 10017.

Science, American Association for the Advancement of Science, 1515 Massachusetts Ave., N.W., Washington, D.C. 20005

Science Digest, 888 Seventh Avenue, New York, N.Y. 10106

Science News, Science Service, 231 West Center Street, Marion, Ohio 43302

Scientific American, Scientific American, Inc., 415 Madison Avenue, New York, N.Y. 10017

Sky and Telescope, 49 Bay State Road, Cambridge, Mass. 02238

Space World, Palmer Publications, Amherst, Wisc. 54406

ORGANIZATIONS

Space Shuttle Student Involvement Project, National Science Teachers Association, 1742 Connecticut Avenue, Washington, D.C. 20009

Westinghouse Science Talent Search: Science Service, 1719 N Street, N.W., Washington, D.C. 20036

REFERENCE SOURCES

How to Use NASA's Scientific and Technical Information System, 1967. Scientific and Technical Information Division, National Aeronautics and Space Administration, Washington, D.C. 20546. This twenty-four-page booklet acquaints you with NASA's scientific and technical information and tells you how to use it. Write: Superintendent of Documents, U.S. Government Printing Office, Washington, D.C. 20402.

BIBLIOGRAPHY

Apfel, N.H. *Astronomy and Planetology.* New York: Franklin Watts, 1983.

Arms, Karen and Pamela S. Camp. *Biology.* New York: Saunders, 1982.

Asimov, I. "Made in Space." *Health,* March 1983, pp. 14–16, 43.

Biological Sciences Curriculum Study (BSCS). *Biological Science—An Inquiry to Life,* 3d ed. New York: Harcourt Brace Jovanovich, 1973.

Ebbighausen, E.G. *Astronomy,* 4th ed. Columbus, Ohio: Charles E. Merrill, 1980.

Greenleaf, P. *Experiments in Space Science.* New York: Arco, 1981.

Guyton, A.C. *Function of the Human Body.* Philadelphia: W.B. Saunders, 1964.

Irvine, M. *Satellites and Computers.* New York: Franklin Watts, 1984.

Lee, A.L. *Plant Growth and Development.* Boston: D.C. Heath, 1963.

McLearn, D.C. "Why Drugs Will Be Made in Space." *FDA Consumer,* November 1983, pp. 18–23.

Mendenhall, C.E. et al. *College Physics.* Boston: D.C. Heath, 1950.

Metcalfe, H.C., J.E. Williams, and J.F. Castka. *Modern Chemistry.* New York: Holt, Rinehart & Winston, 1982.

Miller, F., Jr. *College Physics,* 4th ed. New York: Harcourt Brace Jovanovich, 1977.

National Aeronautics and Space Administration (NASA). *Educational Briefs for the Classroom,* EB-82-3.

_____*Materials Processing in Space: Early Experiments,* SP-443.

_____*How to Use NASA's Scientific and Technical Information System,* 1967.

_____*Skylab—A Guidebook,* EP-107.

_____*Skylab Experiments—Volume 6: Mechanics,* EP-115.

_____*Skylab Experiments—Volume 7: Living and Working in Space,* EP-116.

_____*Spacelab,* EP-165.

_____*Spacelab 1 Experiments.* Marshall Space Flight Center, 15M983.

_____*Space Resources for Teachers—Biology,* EP-50.

_____*Space Resources for Teachers—Chemistry,* EP-87.

Rutherford, J.F., G. Holton, and F.G. Watson. *The Project Physics Course Text.* New York: Holt, Rinehart & Winston, 1970.

Sosin, M., and J. Clark. *Through the Fish's Eye.* New York: Harper & Row, 1973.

Tarbuck, E.J., and F.K. Lutgens. *Earth Science.* Columbus, Ohio: Charles E. Merrill, 1982.

Vogt, G. *The Space Shuttle: Projects for Young Scientists.* New York: Franklin Watts, 1983.

Wold, A.L. *Computers in Space.* New York: Franklin Watts, 1984.

Note: National Aeronautics and Space Administration (NASA) publications can be obtained from the Superintendent of Documents, U.S. Government Printing Office, Washington, D.C. 20402. Use the document number which appears in the bibliography when ordering.

INDEX

ABOUT THE
AUTHORS

David McKay teaches high school chemistry and physical science in Wisconsin, where he was also born. He has advised three students who received regional honors in the Space Shuttle Student Involvement Project; two of these went on to become national winners. In 1984, he received the National Space Club Educator Award. Dave devotes a good deal of his energies to motivating students to become interested in careers in science and computers.

Bruce Smith also teaches science in Wisconsin. He is active in professional organizations such as the National Science Teachers Association, the Wisconsin Society of Science Teachers, and the American Chemical Society's Division of Chemical Education. Bruce makes presentations on science education at conventions and has written several articles in the field.

Space Science Projects for Young Scientists is the first book Bruce and David have written for Franklin Watts.